PETE & DUD

AN ILLUSTRATED BIOGRAPHY

PETE & DUD

AN ILLUSTRATED BIOGRAPHY

Alexander Games

André Deutsch Ltd is a subsidiary of VCI plc

www.vci.co.uk

Design: **Neal Townsend** for **Essential**
Picture research: **Karen Tucker** for **Essential**

First published in Great Britain in 1999 by
Chameleon Books
an imprint of André Deutsch Ltd
76 Dean Street
London W1B 5HA

Printed in Italy by Officine Grafiche
DeAgostini

Reprographics by Jade Reprographics

A catalogue record for this book is available
from the British Library

ISBN 0 233 99642 7

DEDICATION

This book is dedicated to anybody with whom I have had the following conversation over the past six months:

Them: What are you working on at the moment?
Me: I'm writing a book about Peter Cook and Dudley Moore.
Them: Really? Oh…

ACKNOWLEDGEMENTS

Thanks to the following for their help, or for their willingness to help: Clive Anderson, John Bassett, Alan Bennett, Ronald Bergan, Jo Brand, Lin Cook, Barry Cryer, Richard Curtis, William Donaldson, Peter Fincham, John Fortune, Jimmy Gilbert, Ian Hislop, Barry Humphries, Eddie Izzard, Ray Galton, John Hind, John Lloyd, Nicholas Luard, Joe McGrath, Bernard McKenna, Jonathan Miller, Rob Newman, Hugh Padgham, Nigel Planer, Harry Porter, Jerry Sadowitz, Sarah Seymour, Ned Sherrin, Mark Thomas, Harry Thompson, Martin Tomkinson, George Weiss and Francis Wheen. Special thanks to Graham McCann and Will Self, Mal Peachey, John Conway and Emma Dickens.

Also thanks to Cheryl at the Richard Stone partnership, James Freedman, Vincent Graff, James Hanning, the librarian at *Hello!* magazine, Iris Hunter, Michael Kuczynski, Karin Mochan and Millie Shilton.

In Los Angeles my thanks to Brogan Lane, Lou Pitt, Erin, Dick Clement, Francis Megahy, Peter Bellwood, Martin Lewis, Frances Anderton, Elyse Gunter and Nina Hammerstein. Special thanks to Barbra Paskin.

The letters reproduced on pages 51 and 146, the press release on page 81, and the audience research reports on pages 82 and 83, are reproduced courtesy of the BBC Written Archives Centre, Caversham, to whose staff I am greatly indebted. The letter from Graham Greene is reproduced with the kind permission of David Higham Associates, and the letter from Joyce Grenfell is reproduced with the kind permission of the estate of Joyce Grenfell. The extracts from *Woman's Hour*, *Let's Find Out* and *Any Questions?* are reproduced courtesy of the National Sound Archive of the British Library. The extracts from *The Clean Tapes* ('The Music Teacher', 'Dud and Pete on Sex', 'Isn't She A Sweetie?', 'Aversion Therapy' and 'Father and Son'), *Derek & Clive Ad Nauseam* ('Records', 'Sir') and *The World of Pete & Dud* ('A Bit of A Chat', 'The Psychiatrist', 'Art Gallery') are reproduced by kind permission of The Essex Music Group. Thanks also to the staff of the British Library and National Sound Archive, the Associated Newspapers cuttings library, Harold Moores Record shop and Jon Atkinson. Also, extravagant thanks to Paul Hamilton of the Peter Cook Appreciation Society (aka scream.demon.co.uk/pcas.html in cyber-speak). If there are any factual errors in this book, no one could have tried harder to prevent them. V-signs all round to those few people too busy or important to respond to my inquiries, or who got cold feet. .

AUTHOR'S NOTE

I have tried to get round it, but for stylistic reasons it is sometimes impossible to avoid referring to Peter Cook and Dudley Moore as Peter and Dudley. This is not meant to imply any personal familiarity with them. At other times, I have found it easier to call Peter Cook 'Cook', and Dudley Moore 'Dudley'. There is, it should become apparent, a reason for this, too.

ConTents

chapter ONE
{Pete's *IntRoduction*}

In January 1995, I was working full-time
for the London *Evening Standard* newspaper
as a feature-writer. My job, in newspaper
jargon, was to write swift-turnaround pieces on
the back of news events. This was meant to consist of
riffling through the daily papers and suddenly having a
brilliant idea, though my approach was usually to leaf
through the papers while having a coffee, and wait until
someone else had a brilliant idea. On Monday 9 January, I was, as
usual, adopting the latter option when the news editor, a man who
seemed to know most of the day's news before it had even happened,
walked over to our section of the floor. 'You may have heard,' he said with the
air of one privy to inside information, 'that Peter Cook has died.'

My first reaction was to turn to my computer and scan the Press Association's
headlines in search of confirmation. As I did, and as the startled features bigwigs
behind me fell on the phones in search of an obituary writer, I noticed my screen
began to wobble. Then it went blurred. When I tried to breathe, a hoarse
snuffling sound came out. I realised I was crying. I swallowed hard and hoped no
one would talk to me – luckily, no one did. We had heard he had been admitted to
hospital a few days earlier, and that he was far from well. But dead? Peter Cook?

A few minutes later, someone barked at me to assist in one of the dreaded
ring-rounds that such occasions demand. I rang Michael Palin, who sounded

Not only Peter Cook but also Dudley Moore

terribly glum. Then I had to break the news to Spike Milligan. He sounded angry, and yet despairing. 'What can you say?' he said finally. 'All you can say is goodbye.' I said goodbye to Spike, wished him many more years of health and anger, put the phone down and sent my copy over. Then I went out for a walk.

Like many people, I thought Peter Cook was the funniest man in the world. Even the prospect of glimpsing him on a chat show was something worth setting one's watch for, and even when he disappointed – as he frequently did in his later years – there was something magnificently nonchalant about his performance which made it more compulsive than some brash newcomer trying too hard to impress. The evening news that day was full of stock footage of a very young Peter Cook performing the Miner monologue, or making Dud choke on his cheese sandwich in the art gallery, or performing the one-legged Tarzan sketch known as 'One Leg Too Few'. Again and again the same old sketches were wheeled out and his friends and contemporaries talked about what a sad loss it was, and how he had not been the same after Dudley went to America, how he had drunk himself to death and arguably never quite realised his full potential. It all seemed to reinforce the impression of 'a man with a brilliant future behind him.' I kept thinking about Milligan's words: what could we say except goodbye, or goodbyeee, to quote Pete and Dud. Was this all there was?

My first contact with Peter Cook was indirect. When I was young, so young that I found Nicholas Parsons only mildly embarrassing, Kenneth Williams was my comic hero and I loved listening to *Just A Minute* on Radio 4. It followed that the first record I owned was called *The World Of Kenneth Williams* and I knew every sketch by heart. There was one called 'Hand Up Your Sticks', about a man who was trying to commit a robbery and kept getting the words wrong. Another was about one man who was telling another, very bored, individual sitting next to him, that he had a viper in his pocket, which he kept insisting was 'not an asp'. I didn't really get that, but I loved the phraseology of it, the sound the words made. There was also a very funny one about a man with one leg auditioning for the role of Tarzan and sketches about misfits, incompetents and bores. Years later, I realised that those sketches, and most of the others on the record, were written by a very young Peter Cook.

I felt a geographical kinship with Cook because my school was in Hampstead. We all knew that 'Cookie' lived around the corner, which provided the opportunity for occasional glimpses of him, often the worse for drink. To cap all that, I had gone to Pembroke College, Cambridge, which was Cook's college, and made a negligible impression as a member of the Footlights Dramatic

Peter Cook: a mature portrait

If you're Dud, I'll be Pete

Society, the club for would-be comedians which he had towered over while up there. John Cleese, who followed Cook to Cambridge, said later, 'Cook's influence was so thick in the air for two or three years you could cut it with a knife.' It still was when I was there. One evening, during a Footlights smoker in about 1983, two lads got up and did a silly, semi-improvised sketch about mistaking a photocopier for a public lavatory, which had the entire room convulsed. I thought it was highly derivative of the later Cook and Moore, as I'm sure, in retrospect, did its writer/performers. One of them was called David Baddiel. I wonder whatever happened to him...

Peter Cook mattered a lot to my contemporaries. He taught us how to sound funny. Years later, when I spent an all too brief couple of hours alone with him, I found it almost impossible to say anything because whenever I opened my mouth, whatever came out seemed to be blatantly plagiarised from Pete and Dud, or Derek & Clive, or an interview with Sir Arthur Streeb-Greebling (or Greeb-Streebling). The man's influence was ubiquitous: like sand blown up by a desert storm, it got in everywhere.

My motives for writing this book are, then, pretty plain: to scratch his name on the desk, to say 'Peter Cook was here, and here, and here too.' And so was Dudley. Because without Dudley, of course, there would have been no Pete, and without Pete, it is difficult to imagine there being much of a Dud.

As I write, Dudley Moore is days away from his 64th birthday. The frailties inevitable for a man of his generation are showing: his one-time mate Anthony Newley died just yesterday and the health of Dudley Moore is the subject of some debate, not to say concern. Dudley's movements are a mystery – even, some say (though his closest friends deny it with strenuously veiled hints), to himself. Ex-wives and friends who have known him from the time he was a virgin – and that was a long time ago – admit they don't know where he is, can't get in touch with him, haven't spoken to him for almost two years. Is he in hospital or with friends? Is his infirmity a media myth? Which is the greater tragedy: Peter Cook's premature death or Dudley Moore's ragged survival?

This book aims to be, for the most part, a celebration of the two of them, in performance. Happy together, unhappy together, bickering or jointly holidaying, Peter Cook and Dudley Moore were one of the entertainment world's most distinctive double acts. They had an instinctive on-stage empathy, and yet they could go six months without seeing each other. They created two characters, Pete and Dud, who delved into their own personal histories for subject matter, and yet in private they often found conversation hard going.

A very unconventional double act

Physically, only a foot separated the men — Dudley's diminutive five feet two-and-a-half inches tucked under Peter's beanpole six-foot-two — however, emotionally as well as mentally they were miles apart. It was a strange symbiosis.

Double acts often make a feature of their differences. From Laurel and Hardy to Morecambe and Wise via Abbott and Costello, physical differences throw up a mass of comic potential. But with Cook and Moore it went way beyond that. Peter's father was a colonial governor who spent a lot of time in Africa; Dudley's father was a railway electrician who spent too much time in Dagenham. Peter boarded at Radley; Dudley walked the few hundred yards each day to Dagenham County High School. Peter was fit, and good at football. Dudley, agonisingly, was born with a withered left leg at the end of which was a club foot. He was extraordinarily gifted at music, though, through which he won a scholarship to Magdalen College Oxford. Peter could not hold a tune in his head, but his quick wits won him a place at Cambridge. They came together to create *Beyond The Fringe* in 1960, with Alan Bennett and Jonathan Miller. The rest is history, but the non-parallels don't end there.

The twinkly-eyed Dudley had, as Jonathan Miller told *The South Bank Show*, 'an almost pagan, Pan-like capacity to enchant ladies', which, of course, led to him being labelled with the 'cuddly Dudley' or 'sex thimble' moniker. Peter, who early on wished he could play someone his own age instead of a 55-year-old, made a feature of his expressionless face for comic effect, and seemed more aloof, even a trifle cold. Both had some sexual adventures – Peter had three marriages to Dudley's four – but whereas Dudley believed in 'the meaningful one-night stand', Peter was essentially the marrying kind. Dudley spent much of his life in therapy and talked about himself a lot, on stage or in interviews. Peter was, to most people, most of the time, a closed book who thought psychiatry and psychotherapy rather ridiculous.

Essentially, Cook was a wit and Moore was a clown. Cook had a satirical or political side (*Private Eye* and the notorious but short-lived Establishment Club) in which Moore never took an interest. But whereas Moore achieved success as an actor, Cook struggled with anything longer than a short sketch. Cook didn't make it as a screen actor, and he said he never wanted to live in Hollywood. Moore became a top Hollywood actor and one of Tinseltown's best-known residents.

Even their vices divided them. With Peter, it was the bottle: in Dudley's case, it was the lure of the Hollywood lifestyle, with many of its attendant vices. At every stage, one seems to be the antithesis of the other. In a sense, it was their differences that drew them together.

The original description of this book was an illustrated biography, but Pete and Dud were such an unconventional double act that this could hardly be called a conventional biography. Many of the stories have been told already and the juice well squeezed. I didn't want to be left having to take, as it were, the pith. Also, few people I spoke to could remember enough about specific sketches to discuss them in detail, and I was left with a mass of words that consisted of 'Peter Cook... genius. Dudley Moore... hilarious. One-legged man auditioning for role of Tarzan... brilliant.' Which was great, but not what I wanted.

Then, in true Blairite style, I thought I'd turn the book over to 'the people' and find out how they viewed Cook and Moore, because Pete and Dud's popularity seemed to operate across so many social classes. I contacted one of the few female members of the Peter Cook Appreciation Society, who vouchsafed to me her college thesis on satire. 'Satire can be seen as a mixture of the topical, the observational and the absurdist modes' and so on. And that was great too, but still not what I wanted to say. And then, to quote the great Howard Devoto, and then I just got tired. At which point, my wife suggested that if I knew what I wanted people to say, why didn't I say it myself? Which was when things started to fall into place.

The result is a book which I hope is thematic, impressionistic and unapologetically opinionated. It tries hard not to be too personal, though nostalgia does creep in at times. It is, in a sense, a primer for the more conventional biographies. If, having read it, you come away feeling better-disposed to either the men or the work they created, then it will have done its job. If not, in the words of Derek or Clive... but we'll come to them soon enough.

Even months after Cook's death, the impression persisted on TV, radio and in the Press that he and Dudley had done their best work in the Sixties. Cook and Moore's renaissance as Derek & Clive received scant coverage. There are good reasons for this, since not everyone might appreciate sketches that contain explicit references to hand-jobs, blow-jobs and colonic cancer. But I felt then, and still do, that the Derek & Clive oeuvre had been undervalued. Even when Harry Thompson and Barbra Paskin's biographies were published, they pretty much endorsed *Private Eye* editor Ian Hislop's line that 'It was rubbish. It was Peter and Dudley swearing at each other in a studio.' For me, and for thousands more, Derek & Clive were a revelation.

Obviously, I was a gauche teenager when those records appeared in the Seventies, but they have never lost their gaudy allure. To hear two famous comedians abusing each other was utterly liberating. They also, I would maintain, enfranchised a whole section of working-class society, giving it a comic voice which had been overlooked by middle-class comedians for years. Back in the Sixties, at the art gallery, the zoo, on the bus, at the library looking up the most disgusting word in the world (which, as Laurence Marks, Maurice Gran and Rik Mayall of the sitcom *The New Statesman* will be able to tell you, is 'B'stard') Pete and Dud are permanent outsiders, looking in at a world they don't understand and trying to make sense of it. Derek & Clive, by contrast, have entered the world, or have constructed their own distorted likeness of it, and they are its legitimate occupants.

Derek & Clive recognised the simple but overlooked fact that ordinary people swear a fuck of a lot, but the way that Cook– especially Cook – uses language is so casually evocative that he achieves something that surpasses mere obscenity. One only has to listen to the scores of imitations which this album spawned – especially, though they deny it, the 'Head To Head' series by Mel Smith and Griff Rhys Jones – to see that talking seriously about stupid subjects is not at all easy, and in the hands of lesser talents merely sounds stilted and pointless.

To give an example: in the second Derek & Clive album, *...Come Again*, Clive (Cook) describes how he got a job as a window-cleaner-cum-plumber down in Beverly Hills, and was doing a job one day when he noticed Joan Crawford lying on the bed behind him. Just then, a tropical storm blew up, sweeping him, in his own words, 'straight up her cunt'. Cook describes the scene: 'The biggest fucking disaster area I have ever seen... Up Joan Crawford's cunt there are fucking fleets of ships, light aircraft...' Whereupon Dudley corpses, but recovers in time to add:

'Hamburger stands...' Peter, without missing a beat, goes on: 'Hamburger stands, but no fucking hamburgers.'

Dudley tries to keep up. 'Well, you know,' he goes on, 'I had a terrible experience with Joan... I went up (her cunt) and, frankly, I was appalled.' 'What,' says Pete, utterly matter-of-fact, 'by the *state* of her cunt?' The inversion in that sentence, with the emphasis falling on the word 'state' instead of the expected 'cunt': to me, that was the comic equivalent of

Clark Gable's 'Frankly my dear I don't *give* a damn' at the end of *Gone With The Wind*. There is much else to enjoy in the Cook and Moore canon — I look forward to humming the praises of a marvellous if under-appreciated song called 'Isn't She A Sweetie?' — but I sincerely hope to explain why, for example, 'Having A Wank' is such a great sketch.

Dudley Moore once described himself and Peter Cook as being 'diametrically opposed in everything'. Peter Cook went further, describing his working relationship with Dudley Moore as 'the worst kind of polite marriage: you sort of sit round, and neither of us is really very good at coming out with what we really think.' This book is an appreciation of that marriage. ■

chapter TWO
{the *HeartbReaker* versus tHE *HomemAker* }

> **Pete:** Miss Greer claims that the brassiere represents the male domination of women over centuries.
>
> **Dud:** Well that's daft, isn't it... I mean... we didn't push them into their brassieres, did we?
>
> **Pete:** Not personally, no.
>
> **Dud:** I mean, I ask you, did we males force the females into their brassieres?
>
> **Pete:** No.
>
> **Dud:** (PAUSE) I've been trying for years to get them *out* of them...
>
> (From 'Tea For Two', *Behind The Fridge*, 1973)

However long you spend in the company of Peter Cook and Dudley Moore, the subject soon comes round to sex. If sex officially started in Britain in 1963, as Philip Larkin claimed, Cook and Moore were among its most enthusiastic practitioners, but their attitudes to it could not have been more different.

The very term 'sex symbol' has a rather chaste quality these days, as of someone more used to looking pretty than getting dirty. For Dudley Moore, who happily screwed for Britain for nearly three decades, the only practical advantage to being put on such a pedestal was that it made it easier for him to kiss tall women. In the publicity shot for their stage show *Behind The Fridge*, Dudley is naked from the waist up, while Cook wears a shirt, pants and socks. The satyr and the satirist, perhaps.

The 'Revue King' of Cambridge. Peter Cook in 1959, aged 22

Dudley with his first love: the piano

Cook's resting state was essentially uxorious, whereas Dudley – being such a bed-hopper – had no time to have a resting state at all. In January 1971, Wendy Snowden, the recently divorced first wife of Peter Cook, told the *Evening News*: 'Peter was never, ever, surrounded by bunches of females, as most of the theatre cliques were.' In November 1972, Dudley told the *Daily Mail*: 'I want to be loved and yet, my God, I am terrified of somebody loving me.'

The reason for their behaviour lies in their respective childhoods. Dudley's parents were emotionally distant, not least because of their distaste for his withered left leg and club foot which required so many operations that his childhood memories are more of hospital than of home. This led to an insatiable desire to be hugged, cuddled and fondled. Cook's parents were always abroad when he was a child, as his father was a colonial administrator, and this geographical distance bred a loneliness in him which was never really cured. He told Eleanor Bron that 'women have always been a bit of a mystery to me', but he also admitted to the *Daily Mail* in 1994 that 'I've practically always been married and I really can't imagine not being married.' In fact, there were infidelities on both sides in his first marriage to Wendy Snowden: Cook was very attractive and he knew it, and women responded to him. We know very little of his early affairs since, unlike the equally sexy-looking Moore, he has rarely talked about them. But they did happen.

Cook may have sought the attention and praise of women, but he occasionally had some sharp things to say about them, on film or in interviews. When Cook played a character called George Spiggott in the duo's 1967 film *Bedazzled*, he told the sexually unsuccessful Wimpy chef Stanley Moon (Moore) that, 'As far as sex is concerned... if you can stay up and listen with a fair degree of attention to whatever garbage, no matter how stupid it is, that they come out with, 'til ten-past four in the morning – you're in.'

By the 1970s, this attitude had become embedded, and somewhat embittered. During the runs of *Behind The Fridge* and *Good Evening*, the show which they toured in Australia, Britain and America from 1971 to 1975, Peter was equalling Dudley for extra-marital affairs, this time behind the back of his second wife Judy Huxtable. In 1976, the two comedians gave an interview to *Penthouse* in which, along with off-loading a good deal of post-tour anger and tension between each other, they even stated their different chat-up methods.

Peter: The secret of success in the States, in my limited experience, is to be fucking rude. The only method. Kindness and civility and everything else was treated as a waste of time. Tell them they're dirty fucking cows and stupid to boot...

Dudley: I don't know how many men who go up and say, 'You're a dirty fucking cow', and then expect them to go to bed with you. That wasn't my experience at all. I said, 'I think you're absolutely –

Peter: – a marvellous human being –

Dudley: – and they go to bed.

Peter: Yeah but it takes longer.

Dudley: Speak for yourself.

Peter wasn't only talking about women. In fact, he was also indirectly describing his attitude to Dudley, since his approach to his favourite vertically-challenged stage partner had always been based on abuse. 'My dear,' he once told an interviewer, striking a self-consciously camp attitude, 'being beastly to Dudley is what keeps me alive.' The novelist Will Self suspected a kind of homophobia lurking in Cook: 'They're obviously supposed to be a gay couple in a perverse way, or an impotent gay couple. Hence the plastic macs. They're low rent but venal.'

They also inhabit that classically unstated Morecambe and Wise ménage of two men living together. Dudley is often hunched over the ironing, the kettle is usually heating up for the next cup of tea. When the tea's ready, Pete says, 'Will you be mother?' One of Peter's main pleasures in life, in the Sixties, was to make Dudley corpse in the studio. Watching the efforts with which Dudley tries to hold himself back and the ease with which Peter ties him up in yet more knots, the tension between them is almost sexual, like an elaborate game of comic foreplay. Dudley, being passive, is trying to put off the moment of submission as long as he can. Peter, the active half of the couple, wants him to submit, and he won't stop until he achieves his climax and makes Dudley crack up.

Notwithstanding the suggestion of an unconsciously homoerotic undercurrent between Pete and Dud, Dudley has never made any secret of his passivity, the fact that he wants to be treated by women as a sexual plaything. As he said in 1966 in 'Dud And Pete On Sex', he likes 'the sort of woman who throws herself on you and tears your clothes off with rancid sexuality.' Dud later agrees that he probably meant to say 'rampant', but that either will do since 'the important thing is that they tear your clothes off.' The point was reinforced five years later in 'Tea For Two':

Wedding day no. 1: Dudley married Suzy Kendall on 15 June 1969

A quiet moment with second wife Tuesday Weld in 1976

Dudley: I wouldn't mind ladies using me as a sexual object, having them satiate their lust upon my body.
Peter: Oh but surely you'd rather be respected for your mind rather than your body.
Dudley: Oh well, eventually, yeah, but I'd like them to give my body a good going-over first.

The image of Pete and Dud is of sexless innocents, cohabiting platonically. And there it would have remained if Derek & Clive had not come along and shattered the image along two diametrically opposed axes.

First, Derek & Clive are both married. But the state of both marriages is either uneasily inert or actively hostile – the latter being most glaringly evident in the infamous 'cunt-kicking' sketch from the third album, *...Ad Nauseam*. Here, Clive (Cook) becomes enraged at his wife Dolly, who has walked into the room and failed to take a photograph of Clive's potentially world-breaking trail of snot. Angry that it will not now be eligible for the *Guinness Book Of Records*, Cook outraged women and sensitive men the world over by embarking on the following tirade:

> "'Shall I tell you what I'm going to do now? I'm going to get the *Guinness Book Of Records* to recognise me as the number one cunt kicker-in in the world." And I spread her legs apart. And I kicked her and I kicked her in the cunt for half a fucking hour 'til I was exhausted. And then I said, "Dolly – will you get a Polaroid of that?" And the cunt wouldn't even get up.'

One either condemns this colossally un-PC outburst unconditionally, or lets it pass as being regrettable and not terribly funny, but of its time. Dudley, who by now had cut most of his links with England, obviously regarded it as representing all the bad old times he hoped he was leaving behind when he settled in America. At the same time, Peter was clearly angry and depressed by the failure of his second marriage to Judy Huxtable. But perhaps that trail of snot which 'Dolly' had accidentally broken was also, in Peter's mind, the slender thread of his eighteen-year partnership – at least double his longest-surviving marriage – with Dudley.

Another set-up equally popular with Derek & Clive was the cottaging couple, in which a well-heeled man – usually Cook sounding like his patrician buffoon creation Sir Arthur Streeb-Greebling, is being 'gobbled' by a husky-voiced proletarian. The first time this occurs is in a sketch called 'Winkie Wanky Woo' from

Cook and first wife Wendy with daughters Lucy (16 months) and Daisy (two weeks), October 1965

Derek & Clive (Live). Dudley has forsaken his traditional submissive role and is the active partner (presumably so that he can make all those disgusting sucking noises). Peter reveals that his penis is about a thousand miles long when fully erect, but that that only happens once a century. He is also keen to know what services are being offered: 'Is it the winkie? Or more of the wanky?' The dialogue tries hard to be offensive, but it's so stupid that it comes nowhere near achieving the desired effect.

Is this evidence of a gay undertone to Cook and Moore's relationship? If there is one, none of their friends to whom I spoke would offer more than a vague, 'double acts do get very close...' which hardly counts as an endorsement, so we should not pursue it too hard. There is also a moment in the video *Derek & Clive Get The Horn*, in which Peter mockingly attempts to seduce Dudley.

Peter: Let's see how he reacts to a kiss. (Bends down to kiss him. Is repulsed.) Still doesn't like it.
Dudley: (spluttering) Blimey! Who wouldn't? Seeing that Blackwall Tunnel coming towards me, all moist and fumey and green... It's not homosexuality I'm afraid of: it's your pongy gob.

This is hardly evidence that Peter was unrequitedly in love with Dudley. Cook's neighbour George Weiss did once claim that after Cook and Moore split up in 1975, all Dudley's girlfriends were at least six feet tall, whereas most of Peter's were about five-feet two. We shall probably have to settle for that.

Elsewhere in the oeuvre of Derek & Clive, homophobia, or unrecognised homoerotica, turns to misogyny — or does it? In the Sixties, Pete and Dud's attitude to sex was enjoyably juvenile, being mostly a matter for sniggering and double entendre. 'Busty substances' became Dud's comically circuitous term for breasts, while Pete excitedly tells Dud that, when they were at school, the playground know-all and bully told him that he'd discovered the most disgusting word in the world. 'It's so filthy that no one's allowed to see it except bishops,' said Pete. The word, as previously noted, was 'B'stard'. Pete sneaks down to the Town Hall library – 'you can only get in there with a medical certificate' – to look it up in the huge volume B of the Dictionary. 'And there was the word, in all its horror.'

There is also some discussion as to what the phrase 'child born out of wedlock' means. Pete is convinced that it is 'a horrible thing: it's a mixture of a steam engine and a padlock, and some children are born out of them instead of the normal way.' In other words, in performance, Pete and Dud were content to swap tales about Auntie Dolly and chasing girls on buses, and rarely ventured far from that enclosure.

In their 1971 show *Behind The Fridge*, Cook and Moore wrote a sketch called 'On Location' in which a successful film actor son visits his old dad. The former has taken his time over getting home, and as a result has missed his mother's funeral. Dudley, playing the father, is pathetically keen to assure his successful son (Cook) that his mother wouldn't have wanted him to spoil the shoot just to get home. By 1984, the tables had turned and Peter was playing the abandoned parent for real. When Dudley left him to go and live in America in 1975, Cook told the *Sun*: 'Of course I miss him. I'd like nothing better than to work with him... I'm really very fond of the little sod.' He went on, 'He is very talented and hard working and deserves it. They are keeping him busy over there with offers of work that make him far more money that we could make together.' Peter simultaneously manages to sound like a spurned lover and a proud parent.

In 'A Bit Of A Chat' from 1966, Peter took the role that came very easily to him as the repressed parent trying to explain the facts of life to his adolescent son.

> 'Roger... in order for you to be brought about, it was necessary for your mother... to sit on a chair. To sit on a chair which I had recently vacated, and which was still warm from my body. And then something very

mysterious, rather wonderful and beautiful happened. And, sure enough, four years later, you were born.'

The speech was one of several witty parodies of parents who would genuinely like to be able to talk to their children, but who are psychologically incapable of doing so. Peter's sister, Sarah Seymour, accepts that Peter and his father might have had an embarrassing chat with his father about birds and bees (as many people did in those days) though he adored his mother and often told her so. Dudley's relations with his parents were more strained.

It was when he was still a schoolboy that Dudley had one of his most bizarre sexual adventures. He was listening to the radio with his parents as usual one night, when a performance of Verdi's *Rigoletto* was played, featuring the voice of the coloratura soprano Madeleine (or Mado) Robin singing her show-stopping (and controversial) B above high C. Dudley told biographer Barbara Paskin he remembers his mother saying to him, 'This woman is singing the highest note ever sung' – to which his reaction was entirely visceral: his hand snaked into his trouser pocket and he started trying to masturbate. His mother, of course, caught him at it.

Years later, at Oxford, the voice of Mado Robin was still in his head, and his hand still in his trouser pocket. Here, though, he was free to indulge his passion by walking into his nearest record shop and asking to hear the song played to him while he stood in a cubicle listening to it on headphones, jerking off into his father's raincoat. Years later, the slogan for the film *10* was 'Find out what Bo Derek likes to do to Ravel's *Bolero*'. Finding out what Dudley Moore used to like doing to Verdi's *Rigoletto* or Donizetti's *Lucia Di Lammermoor* is rather less well known, but equally intriguing.

Years before his discovery by Hollywood, Dudley had been in training for his role as a sexual athlete. The cast of *Beyond The Fringe* were amazed at his rampant behaviour and looked on with awe – and some envy – at the women who made a beeline for his dressing room. Dudley may have been making up for feeling less important to the production than the other three members, who he felt had more input into the show, but he never dropped the habit. Years later, on the tour of America, a 'tired and emotional' Peter Cook was eaten up with anxiety at having left Judy in the bar with Dudley, and was convinced his dressing-room partner was getting it on with his bedroom partner. He tried for some time to find them, but was too drunk to press the right button on the lift. When he eventually emerged, he burst in upon them, dressed only in his underpants, and found Dudley innocently playing the piano to Judy and several other women.

To be the girlfriend of the younger, mostly sober Peter Cook meant joining the pantomime that followed him around, or that he created wherever he went. One watched, listened, laughed and admired. Bedding Dudley, on the other hand, though hugely entertaining, also meant becoming part of a therapeutic process because taking his clothes off revealed the deformed foot onto which Dudley had projected all his feelings of self-loathing. So by sharing his bed one shared his secrets, woes, hopes and fears, and this was inevitably a more private process.

By the time he got to star in the Blake Edwards film *10*, Dudley was being referred to as 'Hollywood's latest and unlikeliest sex symbol'. In the

Cook and third wife Lin, whom he married in November 1989

early 1980s, Dudley was solidly established as one of the sexiest men in America. Newspaper articles were analysing 'What makes girls fall for Cuddly Dudley?' By 1982 he could name Julie Christie, Jane Fonda, Faye Dunaway, Raquel Welch, Vanessa Redgrave, Gina Lollobrigida and Susan George as past conquests – and, alas, could also reflect on two failed marriages, to Suzy Kendall and Tuesday Weld respectively.

To the British Press, Dudley's sex appeal always had that 'unlikely' tag about it, and the fact that he seemed unable to make a success of his marriages was a further jab. All of which only made Dudley try even harder to prove them wrong. Even in 1994, with his latest chance for a happy and meaningful relationship shot to pieces after the collapse of his marriage to Brogan Lane, he was determined to make a success of his fourth marriage, to Nicole Rothschild. 'He's truly the gentlest, kindest, most honest man I know,' she told reporters on 13 April, two days before wedding number four, despite bearing – and showing – marks on her neck which led to some lurid and unfounded speculation among reporters about what was taking place behind closed doors. While Peter Cook's domestic life settled down into a more comfortable pattern when he married Lin Chong in 1989, Dudley seemed to be going in the other direction.

The imagined domestic heat of Dudley's married life stands in ironic contrast to the spats extemporised between himself and Peter on the three Derek & Clive albums, released between 1976 and 1978. These shock LPs cast Dudley in a very different light from the cuddly image which had sustained him throughout the Sixties. In private, Dudley was much filthier-minded than his public image, and Derek & Clive reflect that. There is a lot of sex on these albums, proving that Pete and Dud have moved far beyond their schoolboy fantasies. Well, almost. In one of the slightly cleaner sketches from the third and last album ...Ad Nauseam, entitled 'Sir', Cook plays an excitable schoolboy again, though this time the school is a boarding school – Cook went to Radley – and the Sir in question has persuaded young Cook to come into his study and 'hop on his willy'. Cook imitates the sound the master makes as he comes (a sound and activity which Moore is keen to imitate, though he is really only the audience) and he then describes the master 'shining my botty' with the sticky substance which the master explains away as Brasso. We are clearly in a very different world from misunderstood definitions of the word B'stard.

For a while, America was the promised land for Dudley. He banked multi-million dollar cheques for his film appearances, mixed with the rich and mighty, and in the privacy of his own home could always turn to his beloved piano and to the view of the Pacific beyond that. But then the good times started turning bad. His incorrigible promiscuity wrecked one relationship after another, and by the early 1990s his film career had been shunted into the sidings. His relationship with Nicole Rothschild had already had its turbulent moments before they married, but afterwards, far from improving, the barometer of their marriage continued to register alarming rises and falls. 'I am easy to get along with but bloody awful to live with,' he once confessed. Estimates varied about the number of times Dudley and second wife Tuesday Weld split up before their formal separation (some put it at twenty) but Nicole out-performed even that.

Pete and Dud in Goodbye Again, *1968*

Peter Cook & Dudley Moore present

DEREK AND CLIVE

WARNING!
THIS COMPACT DISC CONTAINS LANGUAGE OF AN EXPLICIT NATURE THAT MAY BE OFFENSIVE & SHOULD NOT BE PLAYED IN THE PRESENCE OF MINORS

(LIVE)

In October 1995, just eighteen months after their wedding day, she was reported as trying to sell the story of their stormy marriage to the *News of the World* for $150,000. The roller-coaster carried on, however, and by July 1996 the couple appeared determined to prove they were still together. At the time of writing they had divorced, and Dudley was lying low. Little wonder that his third wife Brogan said that he was 'always playing the role of a victim.'

For a while, Dudley the sex symbol became a suspected wife-beater, although it was a charge which was later withdrawn and which Dudley always strongly denied. Nicole let it be known in an interview with Glenys Roberts in July 1998, that after their marriage Dudley, 'Never touched me again', which for a man who could talk about little else was a shattering change in fortunes. This was the man who had told *Playboy* magazine in 1982: 'What else is there to live for? Chinese food and women. There *is* nothing else... I don't give a shit about anything else.' That quote prompted the British Press to conclude that Dudley had turned into the same sort of West Coast bimbo that he was said to be dating. Now, though, it looked as if Dudley had reluctantly been forced to once more don the nun's habit which he and Peter had worn in their 1967 film *Bedazzled*.

To make things worse, Nicole's former husband Charles was HIV-positive, and although Nicole wanted children with Dudley, Nicholas Anthony Moore, who was born in July 1995, was a test-tube baby. It didn't end there. Nicole later claimed in court papers that Dudley paid prostitutes up to £5,000 a month. In response, Dudley filed papers at the same Santa Monica courthouse claiming that 'Nicole's allegations regarding drugs and hookers are absolutely not true'. The whole, sorry affair sadly mirrored the fact that some years earlier, in the 1970s, Peter Cook – no longer resembling the 'gazelle-slim elfin beauty, very slim, very slender' as he once described his ideal woman – was notorious at

Private Eye and elsewhere for his attendance at Soho massage parlours, though quite how far he went once inside was a matter for conjecture. It broke up the day and gave him something to talk about. The playful impotence of Pete and Dud – stealthily looking up rude words in the dictionary – had become a reality.

Both men had occasionally indulged in some fairly seedy habits. In the years after their split in 1975, Cook never made any secret of the fact that he would have been happy to get back together with Dudley. By contrast Dudley positively basked in his new life, and seemed to relish being able to remember less and less of his mother country. But perhaps Dudley found it harder to split up than he let on. As Cook's death grew ever more likely in the early 1990s, Dudley teamed up with someone who would possibly bring to mind his old comedy partner.

In a sense, Derek had married Clive. Dudley and Nicole had a fiery, passionate relationship in which he played second lead. They seemed locked into a pattern of acrimonious splits and emotional reunions. Finally, Dudley and Nicole could no more live peacefully together than Derek and Clive could. But they had their moments.

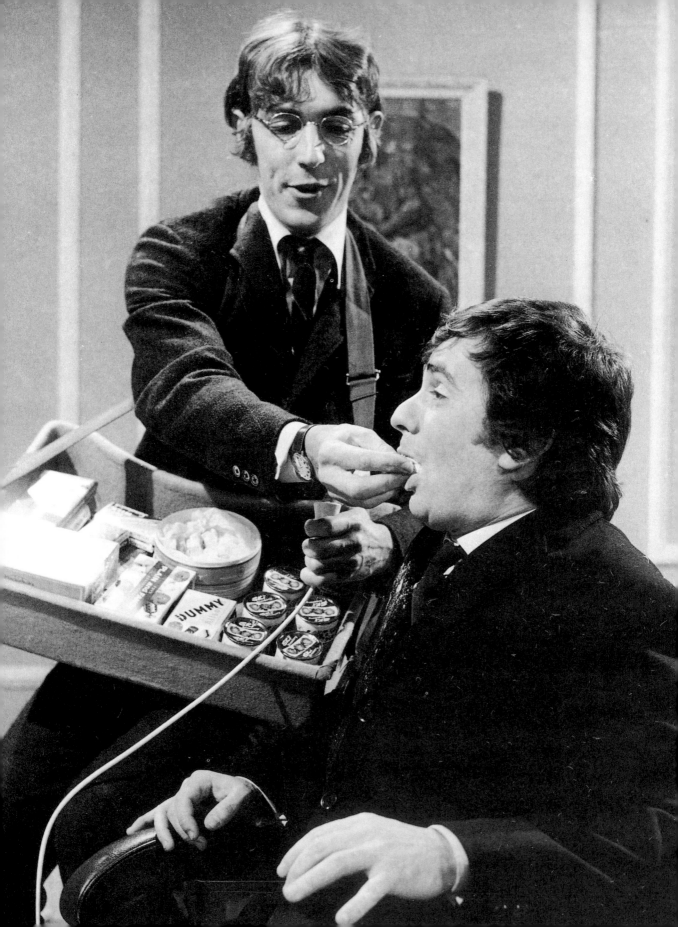

chapter tHree
{keePing *it* in VERSUS *letting* It Out }

Peter Cook: 'I don't know why Dudley keeps on trying to find himself. I found him years ago.'

Dudley Moore: 'He didn't like them, he didn't respect them and he told them lies.'
(On Cook's attitude to psychotherapy)

Throughout his life, Dudley Moore worked hard at self-discovery, whether through psychiatry, psychoanalysis or psychotherapy. 'I've never seen anyone work so hard at trying to come to this understanding of why he was the way he was,' his girlfriend Susan Anton told Barbra Paskin. Peter Cook's attitude was the complete antithesis. He regarded therapy with undisguised suspicion and rarely passed up the chance to deride it. When Dudley went in for therapy, he jumped in with both feet (which was part of the reason he was there in the first place). Peter dipped his toe in the water and then pulled back.

For Dudley, therapy was concomitant with first love. He got into it at quite a young age, when he was feeling insecure and vulnerable and in pain from the break-up of his first serious relationship, with Celia Hammond, towards the end of 1963. Dudley's need to talk about himself was, perversely, his way of making contact with other people, an instinct that had been stifled since childhood. He told the *Sunday Telegraph* magazine some years later that when his mother first

'Pleasure, pleasure, pleasure...' Peter introduces Dudley to 'Aversion Therapy' in 1968

saw her new baby with a club foot and withered left leg, 'she wanted to kill me'. Dudley's childhood memories are a blur of paediatric wards and lengthy operations in which his foot was repeatedly broken and prised round so that it faced roughly the right direction. During his periods in hospital, he got so used to being at least six feet away from the nearest bed occupant that when he returned to a world in which people were actually brushing against him, it was almost too much to handle.

The thing most missing in Dudley's life was tenderness, which was why, when a friendly nurse offered to give him a goodnight kiss one Christmas, he savoured the moment for the rest of his life. 'I had a goodnight kiss from a nurse called Pat,' he recalled. 'It was my first taste of real, unqualified, uncomplicated affection, and in many ways my entire life is based on searching for and recapturing that moment.'

Nothing quite so harrowing disturbed Peter Cook's childhood, though he did once feel ill and was bathed, nude, by the school matron. 'During the course of this she soaped my back with her bare hands,' he wrote in the *Daily Mail* in 1977. 'This innocent action caused me severe pleasure and embarrassment which I disguised with a large sponge.' In Peter's case, the incident, far from coming to represent an isolated moment of kindness in an otherwise dark and unfriendly world, was blown up out of all proportion and an exaggerated version of events was shared with his schoolfriends.

Peter Cook enjoyed a close relationship with both his parents when he saw them, which wasn't as often as he would have liked, due to their colonial duties in Nigeria, Gibraltar and Libya. At the end of school holidays, there were tears at parting, but Peter bore them with the fortitude which the boarding-school classes instilled in their pupils. As for Dudley's parents, his father Jock was a distant and unemotional man, whom Dudley remembers more for what he didn't say than what he did. Moore Senior was an electrician for Stratford East Railway, and he earned five pounds a week. Dudley's mother Ada, the woman who was to exert such a strong influence on him, was emotionally frigid. 'Ada and Jock unquestionably loved their children, but they were so emotionally repressed that they were unable to express it,' says Paskin.

WILLIAM DONALDSON AND DONALD ALBERY PRESENT

BEYOND THE FRINGE

Alan BENNETT   Peter COOK   Jonathan MILLER   Dudley MOORE

Years later, when Dudley Moore the film star returned to Dagenham to see his old mum, he took his then girlfriend Susan Anton with him. Susan was a sensitive and compassionate woman who wanted the best for Dudley, and she was struck, as visiting Americans often are, by the restraint between mother and son. 'I think he wanted to run and grab her but didn't feel he ever could,' she told Paskin. 'He was too afraid of the reaction – who knows, she might have grabbed him back.' The effect of that inexplicably withheld love was to make Dudley think he had done something to bring about its removal, and the quest to understand why has occupied him throughout his life.

Dudley's colleagues on *Beyond The Fringe* treated his ventures into psychoanalysis with the same amused disdain, or 'benign contempt' (Cook's phrase) with which they had at first greeted his contributions to the show. Certainly Dudley didn't help himself. On the set of *Not Only... But Also*, his pained efforts to explain to a group of cameramen that the reason he produced scripts so slowly and painfully was because of inadequate potty training can only have been met with expressions ranging from incredulity to scorn. If Peter hadn't been dead against psychoanalysis already, that would have made him redouble his determination not to sink into introspection himself. If anything, the harder Dudley tried to find himself, the harder Peter tried to lose himself.

Cook's stand against analysis underwent a minor blip towards the end of his first marriage to Wendy, after he had moved in with the woman who was to become his second wife, Judy Huxtable. Relations with both women were spiralling out of control, crockery was being smashed at an alarming rate and so for once Moore's recommendation that they should visit Dr Stephen Sebag-Montefiore of Kensington was taken up. The problem was, Peter tried to outsmart Sebag-Montefiore, which sent each session rattling off in totally the wrong direction. Peter thought he was cleverly debunking the whole process, but his attitude drove Dudley mad. Dudley told Harry Thompson: 'He used to come back and say, "I bluffed him," and I'd say, "How can he know anything about you then? What is the point?"'

Cook's deep-rooted resistance to opening up derived from his family, from what Thompson calls 'the importance of not burdening others with one's own trivial problems.' The immortal monologist EL Wisty was one of the most boring men on Earth, but Cook's gift was to parade his utter tediousness and in so doing make it funny. That was his way of dealing with drones. 'He wasn't one to confide,' said Richard Ingrams. 'He probably thought we might find it boring.' Perhaps, as some have suggested, he was reluctant to look at himself too closely for fear of what he might find.

Not surprisingly, Cook's aversion to therapy was reflected in several sketches for *Not Only… But Also*. One sketch is even called 'Aversion Therapy', and it is no surprise that Peter took the role of the shrink and Dudley that of the patient, Mr Withersgill. Peter's attitude to the profession is made pretty clear from the start: 'Ah Mr Withersgill, come in five guineas, sit down ten guineas, how are you fifteen guineas.'

Withersgill reveals that he has been married for seven years and has a wife and two lovely children, but that for the last four years he has been having an affair with his secretary Jane. The psychiatrist decides on a course of aversion therapy, in which he will administer an electric shock to Dudley each time he thinks of his secretary, and lets him gorge himself on Turkish Delight whenever he thinks of his wife. Cook and Moore are marvellous in their roles, although while Dudley is describing, in mildly coded form, exactly what has gone wrong in his relationships so far, Peter reveals nothing except his contempt for the profession. In another sketch, 'The Psychiatrist', Peter plays the heavily dandified psychiatrist – Dr Braintree – and Dudley plays the patient, Roger. Roger begins by saying how 'in the pink' he is feeling. Dr Braintree responds hollowly, 'Oh this is terrific.'

> **Roger:** It's funny, really, you know. If anybody had told me that talking to psychiatrists would have helped me at all I'd have laughed in their faces, but I can honestly say that our little chats together have really been of tremendous benefit to me.
>
> **Dr Braintree:** I'm so glad, Roger. Of course a lot of people are instinctively very suspicious of psychiatry and possibly, you know, with reason, but it can help in times…

Dud and parents at the premiere of Thirty Is A Dangerous Age, Cynthia *in 1968.*
The cardboard model is of Suzy Kendall

Roger reveals that his main grounds for satisfaction derive from his greater confidence with the opposite sex. 'You're less inhibited are you?' prompts the good doctor. 'Oh, I should say,' says Roger, which elicits an appreciative laugh from the studio audience. When it emerges that Roger is in love, the psychiatrist showers praise on him. When Roger then delivers his bombshell admission, Dr Braintree responds with radiant calm: 'Oh you're in love with my wife Stephanie? Well, this is a perfectly understandable thing, Roger. She's a very attractive woman, I married her myself, I don't see why you should feel upset about that.'

Roger: But, she's in love with me.
Dr Braintree: Well, this again is perfectly understandable, Roger. I mean, you're a perfectly attractive human being...'

Goodbye Again, *again*

Each time, the patient's attempts to shock his psychiatrist are met with stupefying imperturbability, as if the doctor has mastered the art of keeping his professional and private lives hermetically separate. It is a brilliantly controlled sketch and both performers are on top form, but alongside the humour, Dudley and Peter's stances on psychiatry – credence and rejection – are pretty evident.

Both men, then, suffered from emotional withdrawal, but they reacted to the deprivation in completely different ways. Dudley told Harry Thompson that he had once tried to confide in Peter when he was in trouble, and that Peter had been so unable to deal with the matter, whatever it was, that they had moved swiftly onto something less personal. Dudley's conclusion was that, 'I suppose I got close to Peter in the same way he got close to me – which was barely at all.' Despite their closeness, Dudley didn't try baring his heart to Peter again.

The trouble with men is that friendships can exist for years based on nothing more than joshing, badinage, sports trivia and the re-telling of old jokes. In a sense, Peter Cook and Dudley Moore's friendship suffered from the same problem. They could entertain each other until one of them, usually Dudley, was weeping or gasping for breath, and that was intimate enough for them. In Dudley's case, confession can also be used as a seduction tool. Sometimes, after a particularly distressing heart-to-heart, bed is the only place to go, but, for Pete and Dud, that was not an option.

Given their backgrounds, it is not surprising that there is such a proportionally high density of emotionally fractured father and son (and one memorable mother-and-son) sketches in the Cook/Moore oeuvre. It is also to be expected that Peter more often plays the father figure, and that when Dudley gets to be father, Peter completely undermines his authority. For example, in 'A Bit Of A Chat', from the second series of *Not Only... But Also* in 1966, a patrician-sounding father (Peter) has decided that it is about time he explained the facts of life to his sweet but innocent son Roger (Dudley). 'Now I don't know, Roger, if you know anything about... the method... whereby... you came to be... brought about,' he inquires falteringly, before attempting to explain 'absolutely frankly, and openly', how Roger came to be, which of course he then completely fails to do.

As a parody of the breakdown of communication between generations, it is peerless. In 'Father And Son', in the same series, Dudley gets to play a magnificently grouchy working-class dad who has been sitting up until four in the morning waiting for his foppish 28-year-old son to return home from a night out. Dudley spends the whole sketch haranguing Cook, only to be rebuffed time and time again by his impregnably superior son.

> **Father:** I've got a good mind to give you a good hiding. I've got a good mind to take my belt off to you.
> **Son:** I wouldn't do that, father, your trousers will fall down.

The common theme in all these sketches is a sense of emotional dysfunction on the part of parent, offspring or both. A father trying to explain to his son about sex is a key moment in the development of relations between the two, but the father in 'A Bit Of A Chat' balloons it into the stalls. This leads in turn to the sort of scene recreated in 'Father And Son', in which the protagonists, now older and more set in their ways, completely fail to communicate with each other. It's very

Ms Barnes – with which the media habitually address celebrities. Dudley was tiring of it as far back as 9 December 1965, when he was interviewed for a BBC Radio 'young person's' programme called *Let's Find Out*. He was asked by a youthful presenter why he became a comedian. 'It's such a boring story, I feel like I've recounted this for years,' Dudley began, scarcely concealing a groan, until finally giving in with: 'Oh well, it's a boring story but here it goes.' And off he went, describing how he used humour at school to defend himself against being picked on. What he didn't mention was the reason he was bullied: namely, his club foot.

On *Woman's Hour* in 1969, the list of questions would have tried the patience of a nun (the part recently played by both men in the film *Bedazzled*). They were: how did you work out the characterisation of Pete and Dud? Were you an entertainer before *Beyond The Fringe*? Is it true that you have written a lot of music? Is it true that you weren't terribly happy at Oxford? What makes you laugh, and isn't it true that comics are often not terribly happy? The easiest way to answer most of these questions is by saying either 'Yes' or 'No', though Dudley gamely tried to dig something fresh out of the barrel for each one.

By the late 1970s, the Press had something meatier to chew on. In 1979, a slightly more probing Paul Callan found Peter 'dropping into one of his lengthy silences and staring vacantly into space.' The reasons were not hard to find: Judy Huxtable had moved to another part of the house. Callan had no hesitation in calling Peter a genius, 'But you sense he is deeply sad and lonely – now that his wife lives separately upstairs.' Callan can only sense it, though. Peter would never have admitted such a thing.

Given his subsequent track record, it is hard to think of a less suitable candidate for the job of chat show host, but the BBC gave Cook a chance, with its 1971 show *Where Do I Sit?* Sadly for us, the BBC wiped all copies of the show, which is a shame, as it would have made for fascinating, if somewhat mortifying, viewing. Essentially, in 1971, after the third and final series of *Not Only... But Also* and with his film career stuttering, Peter wasn't sure what to try next, so when the BBC's new Head of Comedy Michael Mills suggested that he be given a chat show, Peter was very keen. Presumably the BBC reasoned that as Peter was a ferocious consumer of newspapers, he was obviously well-informed; he was also a sparkling and witty chat show guest, so why not reverse the process? Cook's main motive may have been that of out-doing his unencouraged protégé, David Frost, who was fast becoming the best-recognised face on British TV.

So much for high hopes. The mooted series of twelve was such a disaster that it was pulled after its third week. The problem was, as Cook told the

Illustrated London News in 1988: 'From the first minute of the first show, I realised that I was not going to be interested in anything the guests said.' One guest on that third show was Ned Sherrin, who told Ronald Bergan: 'Being a chat show host is pretty negligible compared with being a comic genius, but it does require certain skills.' And to paraphrase the critic Ronald Bergan's verdict: Terry Wogan asking Peter Cook questions – success. Peter Cook asking Terry Wogan questions – disaster.

In retrospect, the fate of *Where Do I Sit?* seems to us like an accident waiting to happen, but of course nobody could have known that at the time. Peter was, in fact, quite a good listener on the occasions when friends came to him with problems; but in a studio he found it difficult to allow someone else that much of the spotlight. *Where Do I Sit?* should never have been allowed to go on air, but it did and its failure was a bitter disappointment to Cook which he tried to laugh off. In fact, he tried to drink it off too.

While Dudley talked frankly, and sometimes too unguardedly, about his private life – so much so that Peter Preston, writing in The *Guardian* in 1998, urged him to 'never give another interview again' – there were rare moments when Peter's bluff exterior cracked and he told all, especially after Dudley's solo career appeared to be on the rise. If the 1979 quote from the *News Of The World* is to be believed, he acknowledged: 'I've made many, many mistakes. I know I've been destructive. What I do reflects the idiocy and chaos within myself. I don't think I fit in anywhere comfortably. From time to time I'm contented, but that's the best I've ever achieved.' And then, most tellingly: 'I do a lot of "if only". Maybe that's me – the "if only" man.' So there it was, as stark as you could get: from Not Only to If Only in ten years.

During Cook's solitary period in the early 1980s, any partner, even an unwitting one, would serve as a listening ear, and he became an enthusiastic – and, initially at least, incognito – caller to radio phone-in programmes where, freed from the prying camera lens, he could take on any persona he wished to create. The starting point for this burst of audio comedy came from his friend and neighbour George Weiss, a fascinating, eccentric and occasionally muddled prophetic figure who has invested considerable time and money – at first his own and then, when all that was gone, that of anyone who was prepared to lend him any – in trying to persuade the nation that it is on the brink of a consciousness revolution.

George Weiss has over the years been banned from most phone-in shows — impatient presenters have clearly had enough of being trapped with George on the line while waiting in vain for another caller to ring in with something more stimulating to say. But LBC's late-night DJ Clive Bull was a more tolerant host than most, and Peter himself had several conversations with him over a period of months under the guise of a Norwegian trawlerman called Sven. Bull soon realised that his melancholy caller was no ordinary punter, but the subjects discussed – often but not exclusively concerned with the problems of finding a suitable woman in Scandinavia – have the quality of chamber music compared with the mass oratorios of earlier years. Having previously ignored the cameras, Cook was virtually dispensing with the audience. Few people would have realised it was Cook and, although his sister Sarah Seymour concedes that Peter may well have been truly sad (in the real sense), he was also dealing with his tristesse in a distinctive and comedically complex manner.

Although Sven broadcast to a tiny band of loyal listeners, the character allowed Cook to give a performance of great sensitivity – a quality previously monopolised by Dudley. Dudley had always been the figure with whom the audience identified. He was the sympathetic character, the human figure who got things wrong, who needed to have things repeated, who had bad dreams that Peter would interpret (wrongly). Peter's comic genius was never in doubt, especially among his fellow professionals. But his presence was too caustic, his gaze too unblinking, to engender sympathy. Like a two-man version of *The Wizard Of Oz*, each of them was missing something. And while Peter's humour was cerebral, Dudley complemented it by supplying the heart.

In the absence of Dudley, Peter needed a straight man, particularly during the long stretches during the night. And while Dudley was in Los Angeles, playing the piano with the waves of the Pacific Ocean crashing against his patio, Peter made do with late-night phone-ins for some clandestine revelations. Dudley had his therapy, but for Peter, performing with Dudley was all the therapy he had ever needed. ■

chapter fOUR
{the *jazz plAyer* versus THE *punk rocKer* }

> **Pete:** D'you know, I often wish, I often
> wish my mother had forced me to learn the
> piano when I was young.
> **Dud:** Yeah, me too. If only she'd forced me to play,
> forced me to be a genius.
> **Pete:** You wouldn't be here now would you?
> **Dud:** No, exactly.
> **Pete:** You'd be in Vegas with some blonde girl.
> (*Not Only... But Also*, series 2, show 3, recorded 23 January, 1966)

Consider first this letter from David Dearlove, dated 16 August, 1960. Though typed, the name of the addressee – Head of Music, BBC Television Centre – is scrawled by hand at the top of the letter. It begins by informing whomsoever it may concern that Mr Dearlove of Key Music Ltd, 4 Denmark Street, Covent Garden (director and chairman one J Dankworth) is now the personal manager of Dudley Moore, and that Mr Dearlove would be grateful if future bookings, contracts and payments could be made through him. He continues:

'It may be difficult to decide where in your files to index Dudley Moore, because he is a solo instrumentalist (keyboard and string instruments), a musical director, a composer of jazz and serious music, a mime, comic actor – and a countertenor.'

Having raised these points, Mr Dearlove resolves the dilemma by suggesting that 'these talents can all be put under the two headings "composer" and "entertainer"'. Mr Dearlove is entitled to sound a bit breathless: he was dealing with a very hot property. And as is evident from the flurry of letters and contracts passing between the offices of Key Music and the BBC, young Mr Moore's talents were indeed taken very seriously.

Consider too this letter from the producer of the 1966 *Not Only... But Also* Christmas special, John Street, to the chief inspector of the Savile Row police station, apologising for a spot of disruption on the streets of London.

> 'Regrettably for you but to our good fortune, John Lennon of The Beatles, volunteered to play a part in one of the sequences at a moment's notice which, I am sorry to say, caused the somewhat chaotic conditions with Press and public...'

John Lennon was a firm fan of Cook and Moore, and he popped up every now and then in *Not Only... But Also*. In another sketch, introduced by Dudley, the words to 'She Loves You' were reproduced verbatim but reinterpreted as a plangent dialogue between John and Dud 'so that,' in the words of Dudley, 'the true dramatic conflict of the words can shine through'. Cook and Moore were on such good terms with Lennon that, a few years later, it was even suggested that 'The L.S. Bumblebee', their novelty single from 1967, was a melodic off-cut from Lennon's bench, a claim which some critics, including the usually reliable Ronald Bergan, have swallowed – wrongly. There is an even more remarkable claim that the Beatles song 'Lucy In The Sky With Diamonds' was somehow inspired by Peter's first daughter, Lucy, which would be an extraordinary testament to their friendship if it were true.

Incidentally, the parallel between Cook/Moore and Lennon/McCartney has been trotted out from time to time, but does it stand up to examination? Well, undoubtedly the spiky and acid-tongued Lennon had much in common with Cook and there was definitely a certain amount of mutual admiration between the two. And the appeal of the softer, more homely McCartney had much in common with that of Dudley Moore. Lennon and McCartney were both occasional dinner guests at Peter and Wendy Cook's trend-setting dinner parties in the Sixties, and Lennon and Cook's final partners had a controversial public image. Moore may have been the soulful balladeer of the two, but he broke with the comparison in one major respect. It was as if Paul had gone off to live in the States, and not John.

Dudley Moore made his name in *Beyond The Fringe* by doing witty send-ups of popular composers from Beethoven and Schumann to Benjamin Britten. These skits were very popular with audiences, though Dudley has often complained that the three other members of the *Beyond The Fringe* cast were not exactly bowled over by his contributions to the show. In his introduction to the collected scripts, Dudley refers to himself with typical self-deprecation as 'a rehearsal pianist'. That understates the range and skill of his musical ability, which his Oxford friend and fellow jazz lover John Bassett must have appreciated when, as the assistant to Robert Ponsonby, the artistic director of the Edinburgh Festival in 1959, he put Dudley's name forward as one of the names for a late-night revue. In fact, if anyone deserves credit as the midwife of *Beyond The Fringe*, it should be Bassett.

Dudley's musical contributions were remarkable, and if it was impossible to listen again to a Church of England sermon after hearing Alan Bennett's devastating 'Take A Pew' monologue, the same could be said of Benjamin Britten after the essence of his music had been re-worked by Dudley. Beethoven and Schumann can probably fight their own fights, but still these were remarkable shifts and a far cry from the 'but seriously though' school of musical interlude which had been the pattern in comedy until then.

In reality, Dudley's parodies were not genuine attacks on Britten, still less on Beethoven or Schumann. Neither was Peter Cook's parody of Harold Macmillan, it later emerged, purely a ruthlessly satirical jibe at the grand old man of British politics. They may even have been affectionate parodies. But importantly, they were irreverent, and approached a revered subject from a different, less subservient angle.

The Dudley Moore Trio released a string of records in the 1960s and 1970s, many of which were original compositions (one album was wittily entitled *Genuine Dud*). Dudley's songs bore titles such as 'Sooz Blooze' and 'Sad One For George'. To anyone listening, it was clear that there was a huge distance between the clown that TV audiences loved to watch, hopping on one leg or having the occasional plate of spaghetti poured over him, and the soulful pianist reaching out to them across the vinyl. The footage of the Dudley Moore Trio shows Dudley looking manifestly relaxed, confident and happy. He was doing something he was good at, and that he loved doing, and his confidence seemed boundless.

When Dudley talks about music, he loses all archness and simply sounds like the passionate student he was. To Clive Davis of *The Times* in 1992, he said: 'There's a certain perfection in everything Bach's written that dazzles me every time, this incredible effervescence. Something like a three-part fugue is endlessly, endlessly fascinating... I love late Mozart, but I can't stand the roccoco formalities of some of the early stuff.'

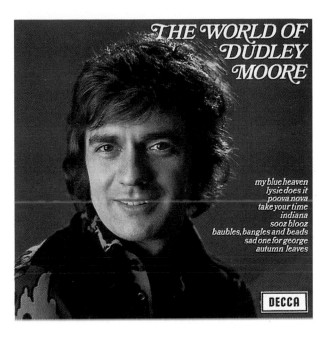

The evidence of Dudley's musical ability is all over *Not Only... But Also*. A piano is often present in the sketches, as in 'The Music Teacher', a marvellous sketch about a wealthy industrialist called Mr Stigwell (Cook, of course) who approaches a struggling piano teacher (Moore), waving money in his face in a bid to learn Beethoven's Fifth (a piece for piano, according to Mr Stigwell) in time for his wife's birthday on Tuesday week. Stigwell cannot play a note but that doesn't put him off at all. He has no time for the humdrum business of scales, theory and practice; he wants to number the keys from one onwards, and commit the whole thing to memory. Dudley – whose small-town Welsh accent is hilarious – protests that 'I can't accelerate the process of musical tuition.' Pressed to accept more and more money for his lessons, he finally explodes: 'Mr Stigwell I don't think you understand: I can't be bought. I'm not some sort of a musical harlot!' It's a superb joint performance, full of pathos.

Music also gave Peter Cook and Dudley Moore the chance to record a song that seems to encapsulate the happiest days of their lives. It was a one-off single released, to little acclaim, in 1966, called 'Isn't She A Sweetie?' Essentially, the song is a parody of a 1920s-style musical cabaret number performed by two ludicrous haute mondistes who greet each other as Piers and Dominic, and soon get onto the subject of a mutual friend, Lady Veronica. 'Seen much of her?' asks Cook/Piers. 'Oh I've seen practically all of her,' replies Moore/Dominic.

Performing their theme tune 'Goodbyeee'

Lady Veronica, it soon emerges, is quite a girl. Cook admits he didn't 'see her dance last night stark naked on the pier' because 'I was watching *Juke Box Jury'*. It is a tenuous connection, but flip forward nearly twenty years and we find Cook once again preferring TV to the chance to meet another high-spirited toff, this time in real life. David Frost invited Cook to dinner to meet Prince Andrew and his fiancée Sarah Ferguson. Cook coolly replied, 'I'll just check my diary,' followed, a few moments later, by the immortal put down, 'Oh dear. I find I'm watching television that night.'

The unique charm of 'Isn't She A Sweetie?' (or 'Swoy-toy', as they pronounce it) proves that novelty records can be art too. The music, described by Cook expert Paul Hamilton as 'a mid-tempo bossa nova vamp', is also indelibly stamped with the spirit of mid-1960s Britain, the sort of thing that would not have disgraced a Bonzo Dog Doo-Dah Band album.

Dominic: The way she sunbathes nude in March/It takes a lot of pluck.
Piers: How much pluck does it take?
Dominic: About an ounce and a half.
Piers: Really? Where does she get it?
Dominic: At Carnaby Street...

It is difficult, in the light of the sheer misery which overwhelmed Dudley in his later years, not to be moved by the sheer happiness in his voice on the recording. Both men truly sound as though they haven't a care in the world. 'Isn't She A Sweetie?' has that precious quality of life before LSD: innocence.

As their fame increased throughout the 1960s, Cook and Moore's social circle expanded to include a good number of pop stars, though Cook, being the stouter devotee of rock, was more interested in maintaining these connections than Moore. The apotheosis of this came in the autumn of 1978 when he was given a regular slot on a new ATV programme called *Revolver*, which was intended as a showcase for the new surge of punk bands flooding onto the market. Since Derek & Clive had been the godfathers of new wave comedy it seemed a natural move, and since – as Paul Callan had earlier observed – Judy had moved into a separate part of the house in March of that year, owing to Peter's violent mood swings and drinking, the latter clearly had a lot of pent-up anger to discharge. History has smiled on his performance as the tuxedoed manager of a seedy dance hall, and it is rather entertaining to see him shouting abuse at bands and audience alike as he goads the spiky-haired crowds. Critics were less sure at the time. Writing in the good old days of the *Sunday Telegraph* before it went chasing after a younger, hipper crowd, Philip Purser wrote scathingly of 'Peter Cook, eyes wavering on some indeterminate point ahead of him, as if reading from a dodgy teleprompter.'

There is a rather annoying tendency these days for musicians who diversify into comedy to belittle their former profession, making apologetic jokes at the expense of operatic lovers taking forever to die, assuming that the only piece of music audiences have ever heard of is Beethoven's Fifth, or making disparaging references to that football song which Pavarotti sang. Dudley Moore had fun with his music, but you never lost the sense that he loved it, and that he took it seriously, which is why his score for his never-ending Beethoven skit 'And the Same To You' in *Beyond The Fringe* is reproduced by Roger Wilmut in full, in the complete scripted edition, complete with every 'sempre accelerando' and 'molto rallentando' as well as stage directions such as 'Look of mild concern towards audience' and 'Look of restrained panic to Stage Right wings over shoulder'.

Dudley's score for the 1968 film *30 Is A Dangerous Age, Cynthia*, directed by Joe McGrath (who had directed the first series of *Not Only... But Also*) is another case in point. The film is a riotous glitter-ball of Swinging Sixties London in which Dudley plays Rupert Street, a composer who is trying to compose a successful musical before his 30th birthday. According to Dudley, he would have been happy to leave it at that, but the film's producer, Walter Shenson, was insistent that the young composer be equally obsessed with finding a wife by the same time. 'I really wanted it to be a simple story about a man who wants to compose music,' Dudley told Barbra Paskin. 'It seemed to me irrelevant that he gets married.' The film was not a great success, either critically or commercially, but it is an interesting period piece, and the music is one of its best features.

Meanwhile, Dudley had fallen into the habit of playing piano with his long-time New Yorker friend Robert Mann, a member of the world-famous Juilliard String Quartet, whom he had met when *Beyond The Fringe* was at the Edinburgh Festival. Nor was he an exception. Many other musicians, both jazz and classical, passed through Dudley Moore's life. Peter, on the other hand, preferred rock wild men like Keith Moon, the drummer from The Who, who persuaded him to record a single in Los Angeles in 1975 when *Good Evening* was reaching its finale at the Schubert Theater, Century City. Alas, it didn't work. 'I conclusively demonstrated that I could not hit a note. If I'd tried each individual word and put them together, it still would not have come out,' Peter confessed in an interview with *Penthouse*.

Peter's friends also included Ronnie Wood and Keith Richard of The Rolling Stones. In fact, it was largely thanks to supergroups like the Stones that Derek & Clive became known. The project was born in New York in 1973, when Peter had suggested to Dudley that they make a tape of the sort of risqué banter that they had been constantly bouncing off each other to relieve the tedium of touring. They drove down to Electric Lady Studios and switched on the microphones, whereupon Peter began describing to Peter the worst job he had ever had, which was with Jayne Mansfield: 'Y'know, she's a fantastic bird, y'know, big tits and huge bum and everything like that, but I had the terrible job of retrieving lobsters from her bum.'

The idea was actually a running joke of Cook's which he had been working on, on and off, for ten years. It wasn't a million miles from the 'bloody Greta Garbo' going 'tap tap tap' at the window pane in the famous opening sketch of *Not Only... But Also* from 1965. This, though, was more than just a variation on a theme. Derek & Clive, the bastard, satanic offspring of housewives' favourites Pete and Dud, had been born.

Derek & Clive caught the temperature of the times in much the same way as *Beyond The Fringe* had in the previous decade. In 1976, there was only one type of music to listen to, and that was punk rock. *Derek & Clive (Live)*, their first album, was comedy, punk-style. It was grossly indecent, a danger to society and an insult to all right-thinking people. It also contained a sketch that had first appeared in the second series of *Not Only... But Also* in 1966 called 'Bo Dudley', in which Cook and Moore conclusively demonstrate that white men can't boogie. Dudley thumps out a blues number on the piano, and then both men painstakingly take each line apart, misreading the coded meaning of

An unexpurgated presentation of an unrehearsed recording session issued as a public service by 2o.

'She's going to groove it the whole night long' and studiously analysing what these 'indentations on the bag' might be. The climax of the album is the magnificent 'Jump', in which the former chorister Dudley earns himself a lifetime's defrocking by describing with hilarious obscenity the scene of a crowd imploring a man to jump from the upper-storey window of a burning house. 'Jump, you fucker, jump' he intones in best plainsong. It's either blasphemous or ribald, depending on your religious views, but it's also very funny.

Music was 'the other woman' in Dudley's relationship with Peter. In many ways, it explains why he was less devastated by the collapse of their partnership than Peter had been. Jonathan Miller had introduced Dudley at the piano in *Beyond The Fringe* with the words, 'And now, Dudley continues to play with himself...' Strictly speaking, that wasn't true. A musician with an instrument may be lonely but he is never lost. Peter was a words-only man: without a partner, he was talking to himself.

As a musician, Dudley Moore has been a success. The Dudley Moore Trio recorded eight albums between 1962 and 1978, ranging from the *Beyond The Fringe* theme to a live concert at Sydney Town Hall. Dudley made two TV series about music, not only with the late Sir Georg Solti (and the Schleswig-Holstein Festival Orchestra) but also Michael Tilson Thomas (and the London Symphony). The introductory programme to the first series was the most

personal, and easily the best. Dudley was writing stage scores for the RSC as early as 1958, and his writing continued into 1996 with a wistful little number called 'Fantasy On A Gypsy Breeze'. He managed a good trade with the violinist Pinchas Zukerman, performing the Beethoven Triple Concerto at Carnegie Hall in June 1983, and introducing Tuesday Weld – they were divorced in 1981 – to Zukerman. Subsequently Zukerman and Weld went off together and were later married.

Since making his US classical debut with the Los Angeles Philharmonic Chamber Music Society in 1981, Dudley has performed with some of the best orchestras in North America and has frequently played mini-tours. Even in 1994, amid the turmoil of his marriage to Nicole Rothschild, he was averaging two concerts per month, for which he earned about $50,000 a shot, and very respectable reviews. 'There were many moments when it was possible to believe that (Erroll Garner) returned to us in the form of Dudley Moore,' wrote the *LA Times* jazz critic Leonard Feather of a concert Dudley gave in March 1989. He also formed a lasting collaboration with pianist Rena Fruchter. She remains one of the few friends Dudley still knows he can trust. In extremis, Dudley feels safest with music, and musicians.

In the late 1980s, while Peter was waiting in vain to work with Dudley again, Dudley was playing jazz at 72 Market St., the Venice Beach restaurant of which he had been co-owner since August 1984. By the 1990s, however, the cracks in his personal life were so disruptive that he could no longer maintain an entertainer's front. He told one of his neighbours that he was fed up with providing background noise while diners slurped their spaghetti. It was as if, in a morose, divorce-wracked way, he had ended up back where he felt he had been in *Beyond The Fringe*: on the stage, but not centre-stage. That was only his perception, of course, but he held onto it obstinately. Dudley had his jazz, and Peter had his verbal improvisation. Ultimately, it may have been Dudley's sheer versatility – a point so well grasped by his first agent, David Dearlove – that led to his frustration at being a musical jack of all trades, while lacking the mastery he so urgently sought. Most of us would be delighted to be a fine jazz and classical pianist as well as a pretty decent composer. Dudley should have been glad to have the sort of gifts that drew sarcastic quips from his comedy partner Peter Cook. As Rena Fruchter told Barbra Paskin: 'I think Dudley is only alive when he's at the piano.' And as the 1990s dragged on, Dudley was at that piano less and less. ■

The proto-punk: Cook in his Revolver *incarnation, 1978*

59

chapter fIVE
{the *wit* veRsus tHE *cloWn* }

If you look in any dictionary of humorous quotations you will find a modest selection of contributions from Peter Cook, but you are unlikely to find any from Dudley Moore on his own. The reason for that is simple: Peter was the witty one, and Dudley was the clown.

Cook's gift for mimicry, learnt at school, reached an early peak in his brilliant portrait of Harold Macmillan during the run of *Beyond The Fringe*. For many people, that impersonation marked a defining moment in their relationship with government, something which, we have been assured ever since, couldn't have been further from Cook's mind. The monologue ('T.V.P.M.') is full of affectionate swipes about Macmillan's crusty air of patrician condescension. 'Good evening,' begins the prime minister in a sort of phrase which even then was beginning to be a favourite of Cook's. According to the script as edited by Roger Wilmut, Cook goes on:

'I have recently been travelling the world – on your behalf and at your expense – meeting some of the chaps with whom I hope to be shaping your future. I went first to Germany, and there I spoke with the German Foreign Minister, Herr... Herr and there, and we exchanged many words in our respective languages, so precious little came of that in the way of understanding.'

There are several brilliant jokes here, especially the image of two senior government officials standing in front of each other, having a full and frank exchange of views which neither of them understands. But the text reproduced here is not fully accurate. In the one recording we have of that famous sketch, Cook actually says, 'I spoke with the German Foreign Minister, Herr...' He then pauses, and the audience, presuming that Supermac has forgotten the man's name, laugh. In fact Cook goes one better than that, producing a deep, guttural sound comparable to that of a cow in labour which, when transliterated, reads something like, 'Herr Nuuurr...' He thus implies that the German chap's name was something unpronounceably foreign which no sane person would be expected to remember. In one syllable, Cook had summed up an entire colonial culture, epitomised in the idea that if you talk loudly enough to a foreigner in English, they will understand you. One cannot, of course, register the number of people who were too shocked to make a sound, but there are plenty of people laughing on the recording of the performance which survives.

Dudley Moore's masterstrokes usually took place at the piano. His Dying Swan routine – memorably recreated on his first *This Is Your Life* appearance in 1972 – was a favourite: he progressed down the keyboard until he had edged himself off the stool, under the piano and onto the floor, from where he continued to play. Unlike Cook, Moore had good reason for making his comedy more physical. Due to his 'heightened' self-consciousness, Dudley's physical comedy was a smoke-screen, raised in the hope that, if people were laughing at the aspects of his body which he wanted them to find funny, they wouldn't laugh at those parts of his body which he didn't want them to be amused by.

Dudley's piano liberated him from having to amuse in a purely verbal way, though of course he could do that too, but the discovery that he could channel his funny instincts through the keyboard took the pressure off his tongue, which is possibly why his taste in humour remained more schoolboyish and pun-based. Peter, blessed with absolutely no sense of rhythm or tunefulness, was chained to his own brain and his own mouth. Whereas the clown has an array of gadgets, Peter had nothing except a blank expression and a tongue.

In those early Pete and Dud sketches from *Not Only... But Also*, what you hear of Peter Cook is pretty much what you get. It doesn't make a lot of difference to one's appreciation of Cook's performance if one merely memorises that unsmiling, unblinking, slightly mesmeric gaze and listens to the sketch on audio only. Cook's preoccupation is language: he hardly acknowledges the presence of the cameras at all, let alone acts up to them.

Dudley, on the other hand, emphasises his talent for physical comedy – clowning in other words – by mugging, twitching, hamming, raising his eyebrows and, occasionally, corpsing. He is constantly referring to the camera in search of the sympathy he craved. Peter's compulsive need to force his audience to yield ('Yield it, yield it'), fall onto their back, wave their legs in the air and admit defeat was evidence of his insecurity, though only those close to him realised it

In his Hollywood years, Dudley's celebrity was enhanced by his reputation for being a joker on film sets. In so doing he reversed the role he had got into with Peter, for whereas he had always been the first of the duo to break up into laughter, from *10* onwards, Dudley specialised in reducing his co-stars to tears by making them corpse. In fact, this tendency started well before Hollywood. Director Joe McGrath told Barbra Paskin that on the set of *...Cynthia* in 1967 'He got into the habit of farting before each take, and it was hysterical. The boy would run across and slate it, and then Dudley would go "Pffff". I'd see his face turn bright red and I'd say, "OK, calm down now, calm down and... action," and then he'd blow it.' McGrath reckons there were something like 600 takes during the making of *...Cynthia*, and even if Dudley wasn't in the scene he'd run briskly across the set, fart, make everyone collapse with laughter and run away again. It was the behaviour of a very happy, cocky young man who has the world at his feet, and who knows that he can disrupt the work as much as he pleases, because nothing would disrupt the film more than if he were to back out, or go off in a huff – something Dudley never did.

Barbra Paskin distinguishes between 'fun and laughter' on set and practical jokes, which she says were the 'one thing he tended not to do'. He may not have indulged himself on an epic scale, but one item he could not resist making use of was a small rubber-accordion fart machine called Handi-Gas, which she says he 'unleashed on his unsuspecting colleagues with irrepressible glee'. The Handi-Gas became so popular that Mary Tyler Moore issued the cast and crew of *Six Weeks* with one each in 1981. Nor were they only used on set. Dudley's then girlfriend, Susan Anton, told Paskin she remembers him signing a check for room service during a stay in a hotel, while all the time emitting a series of fart sounds, to the discomfort of the attendant bellboy. It is hard to imagine Peter Cook amusing himself by creating the suspicion in other people's mind that he had broken wind.

During the making of *Unfaithfully Yours* in 1983, Dudley's deployment of Handi-Gas was so effective that he reduced his leading lady Nastassja Kinski to tears: on one occasion she laughed so hard that she wet her pants.

According to Paskin, Dudley was himself reduced to helpless laughter on the set of *Blame It On The Bellboy*, which he started work on in April 1991. During filming, his co-star Bronson Pinchot told him a story about a production of *The Sound Of Music* in which the last two words of the Mother Superior's question to Maria – 'What is it you can't face?' – came across as 'cunt-face', with predictably hilarious consequences.

The physicality of his comedy is one reason why Dudley has so often been compared to Peter Sellers. Some go further, likening him to Charlie Chaplin. The British composer Leslie Bricusse, who became a close friend of Dudley's in Hollywood, extends the net to include Tony Newley and Ron Moody. Bricusse once saw Moore and Newley being interviewed together. 'It was amazing,' he said. 'They were like brothers. Their mannerisms, their style, even the way they spoke were so similar, and I felt this strange, dark streak that ran through them related them perfectly. They were both basically pessimists and brilliant clowns who went through morose times.'

And what of Peter Cook? It's hard to imagine Cook delighting in something as juvenile as a fart machine, though as a topic (as we shall see) it was not one he skirted – or squirted – round. Cook undertook his fair share of japes, but they were of a different nature. According to Harry Thompson, he enjoyed improvising elaborate games like playing candle-lit table tennis against Spike Milligan in his garage with two six-foot builders' planks. Then there was the elaborate and bizarre method by which he took revenge on Robert Maxwell. The old crook had launched one of his many attempts to quash Cook's beloved *Private Eye* in 1986, by printing a parody that had the supremely witty title of *Not Private Eye*. While editor Ian Hislop and others fretted over how to get hold of the dummy issue, Cook's solution was to send a crate of whisky over to the four drones who had been dragooned into writing it. A few hours later, an *Eye* crack squad led by Cook walked calmly into Maxwell's office, scrawled 'Hello Captain Bob' all over the walls, eased the dummy from the hands of the plastered hacks, and even phoned Maxwell himself in his apartment in New York. And that, essentially, was how to get one's own back on bent tycoons.

So much for Cook the stuntman. For Cook the performer, the word was all-important. Even though it was said he was never seen in public with a book, at home he read them avidly. He also devoured newspapers and magazines as greedily as cigarettes – and he could keep more than one newspaper on the go at the same time. They informed his contributions to topical news programmes like *The News Quiz* and, less successfully, *Have I Got News For You*. His famous parody of the judge's summing-up speech from the Jeremy Thorpe trial at the first Amnesty International Show (aka *The Secret Policeman's Ball*) in 1979 included the blissfully destructive description of a 'Mr Norman St John Scott' (aka Norman Scott) as 'a self-confessed player of the pink oboe'. As Michael Palin recalls in his contribution to Lin Cook's book, *Something Like Fire*, Cook was still working on the speech in the wings as he waited to go on, and he asked if anyone could provide him with an

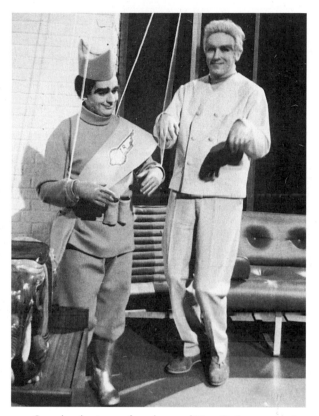

Superthunderstingcar: from the second Not Only..., *1966*

interesting alternative word for 'homosexual'. Billy Connolly remembered having heard the phrase 'player of the pink oboe'. It was Cook, though, who refined it yet further by adding 'self-confessed'. 'It was the "self-confessed" that made me laugh most of all,' says Palin.

Cook's way with words was all too apparent to the other three members of the prospective *Beyond The Fringe* show from their first meeting in an Italian restaurant in 1960. Dudley, being shy and somewhat awestruck by his fellow performers, was slow to make an impression, but is chiefly remembered for walking in and out of the doors to the kitchen behind the waitresses while doing an impersonation of Groucho Marx. Regrettably, whatever Cook actually said on that occasion has been lost forever, vanished without trace. Dudley, by doing his Groucho walk, left a more concrete image for those of us who could not be there.

1979: Dudley hits the Bo time in 10

Cook's wordplay was central to the success of *Not Only... But Also*. In 'Art Gallery', Cook reduces Dudley to shoulder-heaving hysterics as he waxes lyrical about the eyes in Vernon Ward's duck pictures 'following you round the room'. 'Both eyes?' asks Dud. 'If they're in profile, isn't there only one eye visible?' 'Ah,' says Pete, 'but you get the impression that the other eye is craning round the beak to look at you.' And as for the bottoms in the Cézanne nudes following you round the room. . .'His main aim seemed to be to contort me into as many strange positions as he could,' Dudley told Peter's biographer Harry Thompson.

After Cook's death in 1995, amid the plethora of tributes to him from every corner of the entertainment industry, one was left with a feeling of emptiness. Many people had talked about how Peter's wit could light up a room, but no one had managed to put us into that room with him. It was, of course, impossible: you cannot recreate something as fleeting as a chance remark at a party. Luckily, of course, there is plenty of evidence of how funny Cook could be on record or in interviews, but one is somehow left with the feeling that it is second-best. We cannot re-enter that room in Cambridge where John Bird first encountered him, and from which Bird burst forth to announce to Eleanor Bron that he 'had just met the funniest man in England'. We can't be with him at the rehearsals, or back-stage or in the wings, or at the after-show party, or at any of the breaks in filming, or at the *Private Eye* writing sessions where, it is said, the more intimate circumstances really allowed his wit to shine through. One can't help feeling that the intrusion of recording equipment, whether a microphone or a camera, and the barrier of the TV screen or the film camera, somewhat diluted the impact of his talent.

The quest for the elusive killer sentence or phrase was like the search for the Grail for Peter Cook. In the 1970s, performance and intimacy crystallised briefly on the three scorchingly scabrous Derek & Clive albums, which were all, except for one or two bits of the first album, recorded in front of a plate of glass behind which sat various technicians and assorted wives and partners. To return briefly to that first album, *Derek & Clive (Live)* – and the famous sketch in which Clive (Cook) describes how he had to retrieve lobsters from Jayne Mansfield's bum – the story is told entirely straight, as if Clive were standing at the bar of his local pub, chatting: 'It was my job every evening to go round to Jayne – who was a sweet girl: sweet, charming, shy, mysterious girl – and get these *fucking… lobsters…* out of her arsehole. Which was so tricky, because she was a very sensitive woman.'

The throwaway phrases about Jayne Mansfield's character which Cook drops into those two lines give it a comic velocity that showed him at his best. They distract us from the image of Ms Mansfield's bottom, stuffed with lobsters, while simultaneously colouring in the scene with ever greater detail.

Then Peter asks Dudley about the worst job he's ever had. Dudley is obviously startled by the question at first, and coughs, which gives him the idea of saying that he 'had to collect up all the phlegm what Winston Churchill had gobbed up into the bucket by his bed.' 'Oh God yes, I was offered that job,' says Cook, instantly taking Dudley's thought and elaborating on it more successfully than Dudley could, 'but I said, "No, I'm not going to collect all that phlegm, because he has *so* many cigars, *so much brandy: I am not, as a human being, going* to go round with buckets collecting that fucking phlegm."' Again, the phrase 'as a human being' stands out. Michael Palin, if he had been waiting in the wings that time too, would have been duly impressed.

It is this use of ordinary dialogue to describe outrageously abnormal circumstances that Peter Cook mastered in the best of his work on the Derek & Clive albums. Dudley, it must be said, was more comfortable basing Peter than branching out on his own. Another example from the same track illustrates this. Cook ventures the view that a bogey Winston Churchill produced was as big as the Titanic. Dudley, seizing on this, whispers hoarsely: 'The bogey that was as big

67

as the Titanic was, in fact, the Titanic,' only for Cook to snap back, 'Well this is what I heard! I've never had it confirmed...' Each time Dudley pulls off a major imaginative leap, he finds Peter already there, waiting for him, at the top.

Derek & Clive (Live) was released in the autumn of 1976 and surprised Chris Blackwell's Island Records by selling 100,000 in the UK alone, despite earning the derision of, among others, Dudley's biographer Paul Donovan. Since Paskin, Donovan's book is no longer essential reading, though he did go to the trouble of counting the number of times the word 'fuck' appears in the albums (105 occurrences on ... *Come Again* and 110 on ... *Ad Nauseam*). It is easy to decry these albums. Harry Thompson describes *Derek & Clive (Live)* as being popular 'mainly among adolescent boys', and while it is hard to argue with that statement, simply to denigrate the albums is to miss a lot of their worth.

That final, late flowering of Pete and Dud's partnership was remarkable because Cook sounded so elastic. He had loosened up and lost the straitjacket of his earlier years. Dudley, on the other hand, with his eyes clearly on something more sun-baked than a smoky studio in Soho, could not match Cook's imagination and so settled for something merely crude.

In 'Squatter And The Ant', Cook's buffer's tour of the North Africa campaign, he tells the story of his friend Squatter Madras, who – armed only with a massive arsenal and copious troops – felt threatened by a distant, crippled ant moving towards him at the speed of a mile per century. Dudley, who remains more or less inert for the first four minutes of the sketch, finally stirs himself to comment, in his own buffer's voice, that the tragedy about Squatter is, 'You know that one of these days he is going to let fly with the most enormous fart', which is fairly pathetic. Cook, though, picks up on it immediately. 'Well, this is the tragedy about Squatter,' he says with immense gravity, as if his friend had really got to the heart of the matter. 'I mean, one has tried to hush it up: one has attempted to put cushions up his arse, one has attempted to do many things, but Squatter, taken unaware, may give fly to the most enormous fart, and this will be his undoing.' Dudley, in other words, in straining to find something to say, opts for that with which he is most comfortable: juvenilia. Cook takes the subject off his hands and effortlessly finesses it into something even more preposterous, and funnier, than Dudley's original concept.

Dudley is rather better at sounding like a dirty old man – a voice last used on the Broadway production of *The End Of The World* – witness the character he assumes when offering sexual favours to Cook's elder statesman figure in 'Winkie Wanky Woo'. This sketch must have some claim to be the first time the subject of fleeting sexual relations between two consenting same-sex adults was ever

Handsome devil: Peter Cook in 1972

treated as a suitable subject for comedy. After some exchange of compliments, negotiations start again.

> **Peter:** When you say it's a winkie wanky woo, is a Winkie..?
> **Dudley:** Well, mainly it's on the wanky side.
> **Peter:** And where does the woo come in?
> **Dudley:** Wherever you like, dear.
> **Peter:** I prefer you to do the wooing before you do the winkie and the wanky. I may be a bit old-fashioned but I like to see a bit of wooing before the winkie and the wanky, you know
> **Dudley:** Alright then, you smooth-talking fucker.

That last line – in which the word 'fucker' is given the full, glottal-stop 'fuh'ker' treatment – is one of Dudley's best on record, although when Cook then asks Dudley where he lives, this simple question floors him completely.

Isn't he a sweetie: Dudley in 1973

Derek & Clive divided the critics at the time, as it continues to do today. The range of topics was derided as juvenile and restrictive. Not for the first time the words 'waste of talent' were invoked. But take a sketch like 'Cancer', for example, again from *Derek & Clive (Live)*. This, slightly filleted, is its essence.

> **Clive:** I heard that George Stitt had, er, moved away from the Willesden area and gone up round Chadwell Heath.
> **Derek:** Cancer?
> **Clive:** Yeah.
> **Derek:** Blimey… You remember Enid who used to live across the road… She's now working at the United Dairies…
> **Clive:** Cancer? Christ. You remember the Nolan twins, Fifi and Ronnie? They've taken up darts.
> **Derek:** Cancer?
> **Clive:** Yeah.

The sketch is a classic depth charge. The laughter from the small studio audience rolls up and crashes like waves on a beach at the bathetic notion of a world in which cancer is at the heart of every event, no matter how insignificant.

In the penultimate sketch on the album, 'Top Rank', Cook as Clive describes a visit to the Top Rank Ballroom, in which he turns his back on his wife, only to find her engaged in sexual congress with a gorilla. His reaction is commendably sanguine. 'I said, "What's going on… Who do I turn to? Who do I fucking get in touch with?"' Dudley's Derek says he must have been in a state of near-panic. 'Yeah, well, I've got pride,' says Clive, who then decided to complain to the manager. 'I went straight up, I stormed up, because let's face it, I've got a temper… I'm human.' He enters the manager's office, only to find the manager stark naked on the floor with an ant sucking his left nipple. 'And I said to him, with all the dignity I could muster, I said, "Is this a way to run a fucking ballroom?"'

What is so delightful about this, and so many other Derek & Clive sketches, is that it is not necessarily the events themselves which generate the humour, but the linking dialogue — mostly by Cook, though Dudley has his moments too — into which the absurdism is set. It is the comic equivalent of the tightrope walker Blondin crossing Niagara Falls, only to sit down in the middle and fry and egg. As funny as the sight of an ant sucking a ballroom manager's nipple might be, it is Cook's attempt to respond to this 'with all the dignity I could muster' that is the real element of genius.

Derek & Clive's second album ... *Come Again* is described by Harry Thompson as 'rubbish'. Again, I think a massive injustice has been committed. John Hind's description of Derek & Clive as 'spouting obscenities as a reclaimed folk language' comes nearer the mark. It certainly shattered some taboos. Just as EL Wisty had raised 'being boring' to an art, ...*Come Again* did the same to 'being disgusting'. There was a time when a significant number of boys in or just out of their teens would have found it impossible to fart without yelling 'Nurse', in homage to Dudley's cameo of a bed-bound incontinent. And Clive's casual statement that 'I was having what basically is my nine o'clock Wednesday wank...' put masturbation on the comedy map, to the liberation of many a lesser comic:

> **Clive:** Yeah, so I was having a reasonable wank; I won't say it was out of this world... just a run-of-the-mill wank... I was going slightly berserk: clinging onto things, jerking all round the room, pulling down all the furniture and fittings and grabbing hold of the carpet, being sick in the ashtrays, really having a...
> **Derek:** ...a run-of-the-mill...
> **Clive** ...Wednesday nine o'clock wank.

Most of the pauses and the repetitions have been left in because they make the dialogue sound as naturalistic as it is. Just as Clive is about to reach his climax, his wife Audrey arrives home unexpectedly. Clearly an explanation is required. 'Audrey, love, I am acting under instructions,' he begins, before inventing a story about there being fourteen members of the Russian secret police positioned around the room disguised as wallpaper, and that 'They have ordered me to finger my private parts continually for the next hour.' Frankly, if anyone could make a description of self-abuse sound poetic, Cook 'fingering his private parts' could, because the act of masturbation is not what he is attempting to communicate, merely the descriptive act necessary to render that image. And if you doubt that, muse on Dudley's follow-up anecdote (from Pete and Dud to Derek & Clive they were always trying to cap each other's stories) about Dudley going to see his mother for a cup of tea and deciding to have a wank.

. Cook helps him along. 'Well you thought it would take her about five minutes to brew, have a four-and-a-half-minute wank, why not? It's a free fucking country, innit?' Dudley simply plunges into the bottom drawer, choosing to masturbate over a photograph of his father (Clive's photograph was of Clement Attlee) and coming all over it; he tries to explain this to his mother by saying he has cancer of the penis, and has to get the pus out of it every day. Which is pretty offensive if one is of a disposition to take offence, but more importantly, is not as startlingly funny as Cook's 'fairly run-of-the-mill, standard Wednesday nine o'clock wank.'

Dudley was essentially smutty. Take this song which he sings on … *Come Again*, 'My mum came into my room and sucked my little knob. She put her mouth round the end of it, and I had done a gob, out the little hole that's in my prick, and comes with piss as well, I had done a lot into the lav and fuck it didn't half smell… ' And so on. It's pretty revolting, and obviously teenagers gasped at how outrageous it was, but even then it divided audiences. Some applauded Dudley's contributions because they were pure, unambiguous smut. It is also funny to hear Dudley giggling at his own drunkenness or incompetence, but once the initial shock has evaporated, we would rather move on. It is as if Dudley has grasped the point that the aim of the session is to shock, but cannot prevent himself taking off on a distortedly Oedipal path. By so doing, he misses Cook's objective which is not simply to shock but to explore language too. Cook tries to temper the song but Dudley persists, 'She smoothed it round and rubbed it up and down… '

It's horrible! It's not big and it's not clever, but Dudley is merely doing what he is best at, which is exposing himself. There is, in the words of Quentin Tarantino, 'too much information'. His preoccupation with his mother, with childhood, and with having his cock sucked are the three central pillars of Dudley's life. And what do we get from Peter? Vocal flourishes.

Peter Cook was pursuing a version of slapstick all his own with Derek & Clive, which consisted of pouring the audio equivalent of custard down his partner's trousers. This was the nearest he could get to clown-like activities. Dudley, whose physical comedy would not have disgraced a Vaudeville stage, would have coped brilliantly with the real custard. It was the theoretical stuff that he couldn't quite handle. ■

chapter sIX
{the *satirist* versus THE *entertaiNer* }

The day that Peter Cook's death was
announced, BBC TV's *Newsnight* invited
Jonathan Miller and John Bird into the studio
to discuss the significance, impact and influence of
Peter Cook. Naturally, with two such high-powered
and combative personalities, there was little agreement
between them on what Peter Cook stood for. Miller cited
Cook's immortal 'Great Train Robbery' sketch from the
Broadway production of *Beyond The Fringe*, and quoted the following
exchange between Alan Bennett as the studio interviewer and Peter
Cook as the head of Scotland Yard:

Peter: …through this wonderful system of Identikit, we have
pieced together an extremely good likeness of the Archbishop
of Canterbury.
Alan: So His Grace is your number one suspect?
Peter: Well, let me put it this way – His Grace is the man we are
currently beating the living daylights out of down at the Yard.
Alan: And he is still your number one suspect?
Peter: No, I'm happy to say that the Archbishop, God bless him, no
longer resembles the picture we built up…

'…a unidexter…' The 'One Leg Too Few' sketch at ITV's Royal Gala Show, November 1966

The Devil finds a new recruit. Bedazzled, 1967

In a fine case of 'perception by preconception', Miller used this passage to describe Cook as essentially an absurdist for suggesting that a wanted man's features could become so mashed that they no longer bore any relation to the suspect, while John Bird insisted he was a satirist, and that the joke was, at least in passing, a comment upon police brutality. Each accepted the other's point, but felt that theirs took precedent. The debate seems to have been resolved in Cook's mind from an early age, and in Dudley's too. *Not Only... But Also* was mass entertainment, with hardly a political thought in it, and yet even a record like *The World Of Pete & Dud* is described on the cover as 'a selection of razor sharp routines delivered faultlessly by the godfathers of British satire', as if Dud and Pete at the art gallery or embarking on a discussion about teaching ravens to fly underwater were, in essence, further contributions to the 1960s satire movement. How broad must we make the boundaries of satire for these contributions to qualify? And was there ever a balancing act between being entertainers and satirists?

Beyond The Fringe was such a success that it quickly became essential viewing by its own targets. It has never been claimed that the Archbishop of Canterbury came to hear Alan Bennett's sermon, nor that Bertrand Russell came to hear parodies of his own style of speaking, nor that Benjamin Britten and Peter Pears came to hear Dudley Moore imitating them. But we do know that when Harold Macmillan and President Kennedy came to see for themselves what all the fuss was about – the former to London's West End, the latter in London and on Broadway – Peter Cook went out of his way to include some reference to their visits in his script, and extemporized the sketch to three times its normal length.

The Queen didn't see the four young satirical sensations in the West End, though she did catch up with Pete and Dud on 8 November, 1965 at a Royal Variety Show when, according to the *Sun*'s Christopher Reed, 'The mink and bow tie audience at the London Palladium hooted like schoolkids, for wasn't it, after all, a college rag show when just the mention of the headmaster's name has them falling about?' Satire, in other words, can easily be blunted because its main targets, if they have any sense, are usually its among its most enthusiastic patrons.

Such was the fate that befell the Establishment Club in the early 1960s. It was an idea that Peter Cook seized on during his year off before Cambridge, part of which he spent in Germany. While staying in Berlin, he went to the city's most famous political cabaret, the Porcupine Club, on 3 April, 1957. He later recalled thinking, 'Why isn't there the equivalent of this in London?', and for a long time he was worried that somebody would get there before he did.

The club – formerly Club Tropicana, an 'All-Girl Strip Revue' in Soho's Greek Street, where the later Peter Cook would probably have felt much more comfortable – opened on 5 October 1961. Cook's eclectic choice of comedians on the bill reflected his ecumenical tastes, from the essentially conservative Frankie Howerd (then down on his luck but resuscitated following his success at the Establishment) to the genuinely subversive Lenny Bruce, who was able to fit in one trip to London between FBI busts. By September 1963, when Cook and company were on Broadway doing *Beyond The Fringe*, the Establishment had folded. A similar fate, and lifespan, befell its New York cousin, which Cook – then at the height of his powers as a near-entrepreneur – had founded in January 1963. The London branch collapsed because Cook and his business partner Nicholas Luard were ingénues let loose in the shark pond of Soho property management, but, as Jonathan Miller pointed out, there were too many toffs on the membership list in the first place. It had always been more of a trend than a serious political base. The dogs barked, and the caravan moved on, though not before Dudley – playing the piano in the basement – had seduced an unfeasibly large number of female well-wishers.

A short while later, Peter's Cambridge friend Christopher Booker told him that he had started a satirical magazine with his old Shrewsbury friend Willie Rushton. Cook was greatly annoyed, as he had been wanting to do something similar himself. The magazine launched in September 1962 but was soon in trouble and Peter met little resistance when he took it off the hands of the original owner, Andrew Osmond. Although financial problems forced Cook to sell the Establishment Club in September 1963, *Private Eye* went on to become one of his chief sources of satisfaction, as well as revenue. Cook became known as Lord Gnome, and was praised by Paul Foot, who joined *Private Eye* in 1967, for being 'the essence of a non-interfering proprietor'. The first *Private Eye* flexi-disc appeared in 1964, with the by now well-established attraction of a lot of funny people doing impersonations of politicians and assorted famous faces. Dudley Moore was among those lending their voices to the babble. Whether you viewed these pressings as barbs fired at the real Establishment or a neat idea for aiding *Private Eye's* cash flow probably depended on whether you were of the school of John Bird or Jonathan Miller .

The only satirical outlet which blossomed with no direct input from Peter Cook was *That Was The Week That Was*, or *TW*3 as it became known. (In fact he was offered a solo spot but, possibly piqued at the Frost connection, never turned up for the first run.) It began while the *Fringe* team were in America, and

Pet & Dud getting fit in Goodbye Again, *1968*

though Cook was furious to see how famous it made David Frost, there was nothing he could do about it. Alan Bennett, in Harry Thompson's biography of Peter Cook, says he remembers hearing Cook on the phone to London after the show on Saturday nights, 'irate because he thought some sketch of his had been plagiarised'. Most of his wrath was centred on David Frost, though almost without thinking he had literally saved Frost from drowning during a party in the summer of 1963. Cook was so disillusioned by the craving for political comedy that he told the *Sunday Times* the following year that he had at first assumed Frost was 'making a satirical attack on drowning'.

While Cook was being a small-time publisher and nightclub host, Dudley Moore was developing a foothold within the BBC as a family entertainer. As early as December 1960 he had been considered a serious enough musician to feature on *Monitor* in a programme called 'Two Composers – Two Worlds', in which his working methods were contrasted with those of another composer, Peter Maxwell Davies. He was picking up small but respectable sums for accompanying other artists (such as Cleo Laine) in the studio, or for recording the signature tune for *Television Club* in October 1961 (£51/15s). By 1965 he was getting fifty guineas merely for 'improvising in jam session' for a programme called *Commonwealth Jazz Club*, and his appearances on *The Billy Cotton Show*, as well as *Call My Bluff* and *Juke Box Jury* (with Cook) were eagerly anticipated. Guest spots on personality shows like those of Petula Clark, Rolf Harris, Lulu and Cilla Black continued throughout the Sixties, when, as the star of *Not Only... But Also*, he could command a fee of £500 per appearance.

Dudley's political commitments are less prominent. In 1964 he recorded a short and rather simplistic script with Dizzy Gillespie for a cartoon in aid of world peace called 'The Hat', about two people arguing over the ownership of a dropped hat. It reads like 'Give Peace A Chance' crossed with 'Ebony And Ivory'. In 1986, he contributed to a book called *Voices Of Survival*, in which 120 prominent men and women gave their views on the nuclear threat. He told the *Sunday Telegraph* magazine he was doing it 'because I'm frightened there's going to be no hedonism for any of us to have'. It sounds as if it was the threat of and end to the endless supply of available women that prompted him into action.

When, in 1965, Michael Peacock, the new controller of BBC2, commissioned the first series of *Not Only... But Also*, Cook and Moore – like Miller and Bennett – were so plainly tired of the tag 'satirists' that they were determined not to include any material deemed satirical in the entire show. As a somewhat bemused BBC press release from the time states: 'The fact that the

Peter gets fresh with Eleanor Bron in Bedazzled, *1967, as Dudley looks on in anguish*

Monte Carlo Or Bust: *bust, in fact, 1969*

show has no real format is, in effect, its format…' It adds that 'Dudley Moore is one of Britain's leading jazz musicians and at the present time is writing the theme music for the new Peter Sellers/Peter O'Toole film, *What's New, Pussycat?* Peter Cook is soon to start filming Evelyn Waugh's novel *Scoop*, in which he is playing the lead.' Sadly, Moore and Cook did not see either of these projects through to completion.

The BBC kept a very careful eye on public reaction to their latest comic pairing. The audience research department submitted a report of the first programme broadcast on 9 January 1965. Overall, there was a warm though cautious welcome from the sample audience; the programme was described as 'different… and especially appreciated in some quarters because it did not rely for its humour on politics, crime or rude satire'. The fourth programme received an all-important satisfaction rating of 79, described as 'outstanding' (and better than the average for *TW*3's final series, which was 63).

There was further support in two items of fan mail from different ends of the entertainment spectrum. The first, dated 22 February 1965, contains an enthusiastic appraisal of the famous 'Leaping Nuns' sketch. 'They were perfect,' writes the admirer. 'I do hope the BBC keep that whole sequence for ever and ever and re-show it constantly. Thank you both.' It was signed: 'Yours sincerely, Joyce Grenfell.' The other letter was enclosed within a note stamped, with the concision of high office, simply 'D.G. BBC' – the director general, Hugh Greene, in other words. 'You and the producers of the programme may like to see the following letter about last Saturday's *Not Only... But Also* which I have had from my brother Graham,' it announces. The note reads:

> 'What a superb programme last night – *Not Only... But Also*. Can't you give an opportunity to BBC1 people to see this? It puts *TW* [sic] and the present monstrosity completely in the shade. I was all by myself when I watched and yet I laughed aloud at the leaping nuns of Norwich. If some stuffy Catholics object rap them severely. I think it could only have been written by a Catholic.'

The writer was, of course, the novelist and former Establishment Club member Graham Greene. The grand old man and top Catholic was sadly mistaken about the religious origins of the writers, but his suggestion of a repeat on BBC1 was taken up, where a slightly different reaction awaited the act that had so convincingly out-performed David Frost and the rest of '*TW*'. Possibly reflecting a changed socio-demographic figure (from 84 per cent – A or A+ – to 48 per cent), the BBC1 researchers reported that 'A not inconsiderable majority of the sample were clearly quite unable to make anything of the comedy of *NOBA*, but the main reason... seemed to be the far too liberal use of the expletive "bloody" in the Pete and Dud sketch. It was a great pity, many remarked, that these two undoubtedly brilliant and enormously funny young men had chosen to introduce such a sour note into this otherwise refreshingly "different", witty and most entertaining comedy.' So much for satire: it had come down to an objection to swear words. The fact that BBC2 audiences 'got' the show more readily merely underlines the fact that the Establishment (the social class, rather than the club) – more generously represented on BBC2 – was their best audience. It was now time to see if they could extend beyond that TV audience, into the world of cinema.

Peter Cook and Dudley Moore's joint film career was not a great success. There was *The Wrong Box* (1966 – occasionally charming but ultimately tortuous), *Bedazzled* (1967 – interesting), *Monte Carlo Or Bust* (1969 – tiresomely zany), *The Bedsitting Room* (1969 – challenging but dramatically sterile) and *The Hound Of The Baskervilles* (1977 – irredeemably dire.) In most cases, Cook and Moore's lines were written for them, which was a crass mistake. In retrospect, it as if the writers of *The Wrong Box* or *Monte Carlo Or Bust* were given a two-line description of Cook and Moore's strengths ('The tall one looks clever and in control, the short one is a bit of a ladies' man') and left to get on with it. The only film from the period that still repays viewing is *Bedazzled*, which Peter Cook wrote himself. In fact, Cook edged Dudley out of the writing so as to garner all the glory for himself. In doing so, he produced a screenplay which, though flawed, is a telling and – in the light of their subsequent histories – poignant synopsis of their partnership. It is highly entertaining, but if it's satirical, it's a satire on Pete's relationship with Dud.

Dudley plays Stanley Moon, a short-order chef in a Wimpy bar who is infatuated with waitress Margaret Spencer (Eleanor Bron). Despairing of his unrequited love, he attempts suicide, but is interrupted by a mysterious stranger called George Spiggott who, it turns out, is a Mephistophelean figure, willing to grant Stanley seven wishes in return for his soul. (The production of *Faust* which Cook saw in Hamburg during his year off had finally borne fruit.) Stanley agrees to the Faustian pact – his contract is filed away just after 'Miller' – and sets out to ensnare Margaret.

The trouble is that he is up against the Devil, whose interpretation of each of Stanley's wishes allows him a loophole that would not have disgraced a top-shot solicitor. For his first wish, for example, Stanley asks to possess a degree of intelligence which Margaret will find irresistible, and is immediately transformed into a prolix Welshman with interminable opinions on modern art. Margaret is enchanted – rather sneakily, her personality changes to suit each sketch – and the pair go from the zoo (where Pete and Dud had ventured recently too on *Not Only… But Also*) back to his place. Here, Bron repeats the role that brought her so much acclaim when she performed it with John Fortune – that of a middle-class girl who talks endlessly about 'freedom', 'impulsiveness' and 'touching', but recoils with a shriek when Stanley takes her comments as a cue to lay a finger on her.

Throughout the film, Stanley is brought tantalisingly close to consummating his passion for Margaret, but again and again he is denied. Of course, Dudley in real life was the complete reverse of Stanley Moon (the name mistakenly conferred

Typecasting for Raquel Welch as Temptation in Bedazzled

on him by John Gielgud after a chance meeting at an airport) in his approach to women. He may have feared rejection, but that was more than compensated for by his strike rate. Peter's George Spiggott (the name of the 'unidexter' from 'One Leg Too Few'), on the other hand, is an exaggeration of Cook: all-powerful and omnipresent, despite owning a run-down club called the Rendezvous.

At one stage, the sweet but slightly pathetic Stanley says to George: 'You know, Mr Spiggott? You're really the first person who's ever taken the trouble to talk to me. I like you, but you keep on doing these terrible things.' To which Spiggott breezily replies: 'It's nothing personal,' an exchange that echoes the sort of 'My dear, being beastly to Dudley is the only thing that keeps me going'

remark which Cook was prone to make from time to time.

There is a good deal in the film drawn from Peter's power over Dudley, and it is Peter who delivers the most cryptically revelatory line in the entire movie. Stanley is complaining that George must be having a great time as the Devil. George snaps back: 'I've lost me spark. There was a time I used to get lots of ideas. I was creative, original. I thought up the Seven Deadly Sins in one afternoon. The only thing I've thought of recently is advertising.' No one could have written that line for Peter Cook except Peter Cook, who was then at or close to the height of his powers.

During this time the two also wrote and made one solo film each. Dudley made 30 *Is A Dangerous Age, Cynthia* with Joe McGrath. It's another period piece, a snapshot of Swinging London with Dudley playing a thinly disguised version of himself as Rupert Street, a composer with fixations about his age and women. Peter teamed up with Kevin Billington to make *The Rise And Rise of Michael Rimmer*, about a market research whizz-kid who rises effortlessly through the rank and file, discredits anyone who gets in his way and eventually becomes dictator after pushing the prime minister off a North Sea oil rig. It was certainly a biting satire about power and about the means by which political impotence is presented to the public as an opportunity for improving their own lives. The character of Rimmer was a thinly disguised portrait not of himself – of course – but of David Frost.

The ridicule meted out to politicians in …*Michael Rimmer* was inevitable, given Cook's hatred of most politicians' capacity for taking themselves seriously. But being a man of moods, his opinions were forever fluid, so that what appeared sensible one day was merely sententious nonsense the next. Cook was capable of sounding serious, though, as when he was invited to sit alongside Enoch Powell during a recording of *Any Questions?*, then on Radio 2 on 17 October 1969. One questioner asked whether the team felt sanctions against Rhodesia should be preserved. Powell – the subject of much lampooning from *Private Eye* in print as well as on disc – went on a little rant about practicalities, realities and humbug. However, Cook was even more spirited: he accused the whole nation of losing 'all ability to express moral views', and argued that it had 'reneged on moral pledges throughout the world'. He concluded: 'I would preserve sanctions against Rhodesia because I think it's an abominable place. I haven't been there, but I didn't go to Nazi Germany either and I didn't like that.' His remarks were applauded.

Making a guest appearance on a BBC current affairs panel show is probably the nearest most comedians get to being politicians, and to uttering the sort of sincere, tub-thumping platitudes that move the listeners to applause. (A slightly caged Mark Steel performs a similar function on *Any Questions?* these days.) We are so accustomed to thinking of Peter Cook as a cynic that the media myth has grown up of him as a man incapable of treasuring anything. He did value things, of course: he loved his parents, wives, two sisters (Sarah and Elizabeth) and two daughters (Lucy and Daisy). He also held Spurs, *Private Eye* and some friends very dear. But, as Jerry Sadowitz proved years later, you can hold very passionate views while at the same time holding everything up to scorn. There is more cynicism and despair in Dudley's remark to *Playboy* in 1982 –'What else is there to live for? Chinese food and women. There *is* nothing else… I don't give a shit about anything else' – than the blackest pit of despond that Peter ever sank into.

Dudley's total lack of interest in politics was a sort of curse, because in the absence of anything to get angry with outside his immediate world, he fell back on himself and his own anxieties. At least Cook had his organ. *Private Eye's* moment of glory in the early 1960s was probably the Profumo scandal in 1963, but when Richard Ingrams was away from the editor's chair and Cook stepped in, he was capable of injecting fun as well as bile into the magazine. He often went further than the mainstream press would dare, as when he fingered the Kray twins as being associates of Tory bigwig Lord Boothby. By the 1980s, however, he was content to indulge George Weiss's Captain Rainbow's Universal Party (CRUP) which polled 48 votes in the 1984 Enfield/Southgate by-election against Michael Portillo's 16,684. He talked about the What? Party, and assigned cabinet posts to whoever was around. George became, appropriately, Minister for Confusion. The Not Only man had changed again, this time from If Only to What If...?, which in a sense was a return to the state of British comedy as anatomised by Jonathan Miller ('Wouldn't it be funny if...?') before *Beyond The Fringe* had come along with 'Isn't it funny that...?'

In the early 1970s, when the duo collaborated again as Derek & Clive, Cook showed that his tongue was sharper than ever, although he was in full flight from the world of political in-fighting. While Dudley seemed to be increasingly serious about cracking Hollywood, Cook, with his film ambitions largely behind him, was aiming his 'satire' (or just scorn) at the Hollywood starlets after whom he and Dudley had always yearned. The Derek & Clive albums were not satires, but they were certainly not mainstream entertainment. Cook and Moore were not orthodox satirists, though they did satirize themselves extremely well.

For over ten years after *The Rise And Rise Of Michael Rimmer*, *Private Eye* occupied most of Peter Cook's waning political interests, though he bounced back memorably at Amnesty International's *Secret Policeman's Ball* in 1979. As the show's producer, Martin Lewis, recalls, 'There was no intention of its being political; it was just a lot of Britain's best-known comedic performers regrouping to do their greatest hits.' Cook, though, was stung by a review of the first night in the *Daily Telegraph* which had carpingly asked, 'But where is the satire?' Like the old master coming back to show the new kids how to do it, for the benefit's final two nights, Cook took as his theme the judge's summing-up in the recently completed Jeremy Thorpe trial (see 'The Clown v The Wit'). We do not know whether he secretly felt as much affection towards the judge, Mr Justice Cantley, as he did for Macmillan, but there was more venom in his address than Supermac had ever inspired. For many people, Cook the satirist had re-emerged, but what seems clear is that Cook did satire because satire was something he could do: he was merely playing to one of his many strengths. Former *Private Eye* editor Richard Ingrams said that Cook was 'a Hampstead rightie, like me', a view disputed by Cook's sister Sarah. Cook's theory on satire, as outlined to Harry Thompson by Roger Law, was that 'you should be completely and utterly unfair' to everyone. Cook pursued all these theories at times, though he seems also to have felt that satire, still less mainstream humour, didn't change anything. In 1990, talking dyspeptically about the Thatcher government to John Hind, he said: 'By God these people need taking apart! They're awful, aren't they? I wish I had more energy to do it myself. Whenever I see anyone young and funny I feel it's almost their *duty* to have a go.'

Cook might have hated the Thatcher government, but, in his mercurial way, he was sorry to see the Iron Lady herself go in 1990. And just as he was present at the birth of Mrs Wilson's Diary in *Private Eye* a generation earlier, he was also joint progenitor, with John Wells and Richard Ingrams, of the 'Dear Bill' letters. By casting Denis Thatcher as an amiable old buffer, the letters probably won back a few thousand votes for the Tories. Cook chose to concentrate on Denis, though, and not his wife, because the voice of Denis came to him more easily in print. As a further irony, when Peter died in 1995, Britain's prime minister was a man whose voice sounded as if it had been modelled on another of Cook's creations. EL Wisty.

When Dudley got the chance to open a little place of his own, it was a far cry from the Establishment. Just a short walk from Venice beach, the beautifully designed interior of 72 Market St. was very different from Greek Street. There was no satirical impetus behind the oyster bar and grill, and certainly no space for stand-up comedians, though with fellow investors like Liza Minnelli (his co-star in the smash-hit 1981 film *Arthur*) and Tina Sinatra, and given the guaranteed A-list level of celebrities who regularly turned up, there must have been plentiful opportunities for satire and subversion, albeit on a more intimate level. EL Wisty once recorded some rambles on his favourite subject of world domination for the What? Party, sitting on a bench overlooking that very beach. For Cook, the journey to California was a form of flight. For Moore, it was now home. ■

chapter sEVEN
{the *perFormer* versus the *aCtor* }

Most actors accept that in order to take
on a part, to learn somebody else's lines,
one first has to subsume one's own personality,
to acquire the humility of trying to be someone
else. Dudley Moore spent years of his life rehearsing
for his part, by being Peter Cook's adjutant on stage. At
times, as in the seance sketch from the third series of *Not
Only... But Also,* Dud was merely punctuating one of Pete's
flights of fancy, as when the latter claimed to have seen Mrs
Woolley (a regular character in their chats) conducting a seance,
leaving Dudley to mimic the 'click' of the light switch or the 'gutter gutter'
of the candle. Eventually, Dudley felt that there was more to life than
supplying sound effects for Peter. He was right.

Peter Cook created dozens of his own characters, but he could never lose
himself in a character invented by someone else. Dudley Moore's own self-
doubts meant that he was more than happy to do just that, although this wasn't
immediately apparent. As Morris and John Finsbury in *The Wrong Box*, Peter and
Dudley were asked to play caricatures, a role which they carried out reasonably
well. Cook was wooden, Moore was life-like: in fact, he was fine, but his lines
were... well, dud. It was a problem that was to recur in later life.

Peter's reluctance to expose himself as an actor sprang, at least in part, from the
intellectual hauteur with which he viewed actors. While the cast of *The Wrong Box*

Dudley baring his chest, Peter his legs, for Behind The Fridge, *1971*

chatted between takes, Cook tried as usual to charm them with wit. The actors, though, being actors, preferred to stay together and chat about acting. Cook went off in a huff and returned to the incident some years later with this denunciation: 'The good thing about a university background is, it keeps you from getting as conceited as most actors. Unlike them, you have a period of intellectual activity. You get curious and you then stay curious. This means you're less likely to become enthralled with yourself than the actors and actresses with no cultural or intellectual background.' In other words, they hadn't laughed at his jokes.

If Peter Cook wrote Dudley's best lines, Dudley was their best interpreter, in a collaboration which resembles Benjamin Britten and Peter Pears. And Cook was at his best charting the differences between himself and Dudley Moore as he did in the script for *Bedazzled*, the film which Paul Donovan unfairly derided as 'awful' and 'almost a complete failure'. When Dudley, as Stanley Moon, asks the Devil (Cook) if he can be as sexy as a pop star, the Devil grants him his wish and he plays a pop star in a groovy *Top Of The Pops*-type set. Dudley gets to sing an impassioned chant of 'Love me! Love me!' as teenage girls scream their heads off. He continues: 'I'm on my knees, won't you please come and love me. I need you so, please don't go, stay and love me.' However, the next act, Drimble Wedge And The Vegetations – whose singer bears an uncanny resemblance to Cook – draws an even more ecstatic response for his monotone verses: 'I'm fickle, I'm cold, I'm shallow, You fill me with inertia, I'm not interested, it's too much effort, I'm not available,' he drones.

In the stampede that follows Drimble Wedge's song, Stanley is knocked to the ground. There could be no clearer paradigm of Moore's openness and emotional vulnerability, nor of Cook's emotional repression. Moore's singing is as passionate as Cook's is dispassionate, and it was this seam of emotion that Dudley was able to tap into on set. It also made for difficult interviews, because Dudley was so obviously searching for answers to the questions being asked of him, while Cook mostly used them as springboards for more spirals of imaginative fantasy.

It was in their first solo screenplays that the differences in their acting styles really began to emerge. Dudley's debut came three years earlier than Peter's, but *30 Is A Dangerous Age, Cynthia* (1968), co-written with Joe McGrath and John Wells, was largely autobiographical, whereas in *The Rise And Rise Of Michael Rimmer* (1970), Cook could not resist taking the opportunity, together with his co-writers John Cleese and Graham Chapman, to depict in coded form the remorseless ascent of their former co-performer – and, incidentally, the film's

One last pint: Pete and Dud reunite for The Best of What's Left Of…, *1992*

producer – David Frost. In *…Cynthia*, Dudley gives a pretty creditable performance as the angst-ridden composer Rupert Street who gets crushes on girls (of course), receives Red Cross packages of lemon drops from his mother (as he did in real life) and is struggling to compose a symphony (Street finished his: Moore never did). It's not a smart part, but Dudley invests it with such charm that, amid the swirly Carnaby Street mess, you cannot help but like him.

On the other hand, Cook's archetypal baddie in *…Michael Rimmer* is Iago crossed with Arturo Ui. The plot may be as linear as his ascent to power, but the role of Rimmer is a gift for the right actor. Cook, though, plays it almost in his own absence, with an annoyingly subdued voice and a thin smile coating his lips that belies any appearance of inner contemplation beyond the next line. It is as if he is faintly embarrassed at the whole business. Cook's inability to step out of his own shoes is frustrating since, in company, away from the intrusive cameras and microphones, he could entertain any audience, no matter what the size. As soon as the cameras were switched on, though, that mysterious something evaporated.

Ever since *Not Only… But Also*, Dudley had known where the camera was, because he was always playing to it. Aside from feeding lines to Pete, Dud was

Dudley in Play It Again, Sam, *1969, with Bill Kerr and Patricia Brake*

Manhattanite spoken through the lips of an ex-C of E lad from Dagenham. He may have been thinking of *Beyond the Fringe*, the sheer Englishness of which provided part of its appeal in the States, and hoping that it would work in reverse. It didn't, and the play was a critical and box office failure.

Personal problems continued to intrude. Cook's first wife, Wendy Snowden, had moved to Mallorca in January 1968, and a year later it was apparent that there was no future to their marriage. By the end of 1968, when he had been seeing Judy Huxtable for eighteen months, he told Wendy, who immediately demanded a divorce – and custody of the children, which shocked him to the core. They were formally separated in May 1970. It was under this sort of marital cloud that the producer Jimmy Gilbert brought both men together to make the third series of *Not Only... But Also*, towards the end of 1969.

The familiar sketches involving characters such as Pete and Dud and Streeb-Greebling seemed played out, but Cook and Moore cast aside their domestic entanglements to attempt some of their most daring work. One of their most memorable sketches was a parody of a Hollywood documentary about Greta Garbo, whom they renamed Emma Bargo. Beautifully shot on film, it includes the famous sequence with Cook, as Bargo, hurtling through the streets of Paris in an armoured car shouting 'I vant to be alone' through a megaphone. Dudley, as Joan Crawford, is superb.

In the last programme, 'The Making Of A Movie' was a brilliant attack on the film-making process. Peter played the writer Robert Neasden (author of 'A Man For All Neasdens') and Dudley played the director Bryan Neasden. In fact, all the characters in the sketch were called Neasden, to the amusement of *Private Eye* readers. It was clear from the crackling scorn in every line that Peter was getting something off his chest about the artificiality and clannishness of the movie industry, not least when the pipe-smoking Neasden smugly announces that his latest screenplay is ready, and drops it on a set of scales. 'Yes I like it, Bob,' says Bryan. 'It's probably a few ounces too long but it's terrific.'

Behind The Fridge, which started off its life in Australia in 1971, was a calculated attempt to get yet further away from the cuddly image of Pete and Dud. As well as causing a major rumpus by using the words 'bum' and 'piss' on Australian TV, the slim show – fleshed out with old material and some songs from Dudley – contained several sketches of high quality. Two in particular stand out because they explore character and atmosphere rather than straight gags, and each draws one great performance. In 'On Location', Peter plays a successful actor who has negligently missed his mother's funeral because he has been too busy making a film with Omar Sharif. The power struggle of 'Father And Son' has been resolved now: Cook the son is completely on top, and all Dudley's resistance has crumbled away. The successful son has relocated his parents to a new house, with an indoor toilet and colour TV, which his set-in-her-ways mother obviously hates. Out of this comes a gripping portrait by Dudley of the lonely father, struggling to control his tears at times – 'I mustn't let go,' he wheezes – and thrusting his old school reports into his son's hands ('Thanks Dad, these'll come in handy,' says Cook, uncertainly), and trying harder to reassure his son than comfort himself.

> **Son:** Dad I feel terrible about not being able to get here sooner.
> **Father:** Oh, now look Roger, it's your life. You can't play silly buggers with your career, son.
> **Son:** Did Mother understand that, Dad?
> **Father:** I told her every time I went to that bloody hospital. I said, 'Now listen Ada,' I said, 'You cannot expect the film company to stop a multi-million dollar production in Yugoslava [sic] just because you're feeling a bit under the weather, dear.'

actual 'acting' as possible. In fact, near-physical paralysis coupled with an acute ability to deliver the line was sufficient, while Dudley wheeled around, reacting and expressing.

The London first night came close to being a wipe-out, thanks to some typical insensitivity on the part of a TV crew. As they were about to start the run-through, Dudley was surprised – and understandably flattered – by the appearance of Eamonn Andrews holding the *This Is Your Life* red book. Thus, only a few hours before the curtain went up on the show's press night, he allowed himself to be driven over to a TV studio to record the show. What is equally extraordinary is that none of Dudley's friends who were contacted by the show's researchers thought that this might not be such a good idea. This proved to be doubly true when Peter – suffering badly from pre-show tension – followed, got completely shit-faced in the hospitality room and, by the time the curtain went up, was lying face down in his dressing room, with a desperate Joe McGrath (the London director) frantically trying to sober him up. When he was finally able to take the stage, Dudley's concern for (and anger over) Peter must have made him seem a bit wobbly, because the next day, Michael Billington wrote in the *Guardian* that Peter had been magisterial, while Dudley had seemed nervous, whereas in fact Cook had been sobbing uncontrollably in the wings – from shame – until seconds before he somehow staggered onto the stage. When Dudley saw the review the next day, he was so angry he had to be restrained from walking out on the show.

The New York show previewed in Boston on 12 October 1973, moving to New York's Plymouth Theater on 10 November. There, it broke box office records for a two-man show on Broadway, and Peter broke the theatre's own record for being drunk as a skunk during a run. Despite the deep spring of affection between them, Judy remembers Peter and Dudley arguing the whole time, mostly about Dudley's right to be joint-writer. 'It really fucked him off that Dudley refused to acknowledge that Peter had written nearly all the stuff, but Peter couldn't do it without Dudley, and Dudley used to tell him so,' she confided to Harry Thompson, adding, 'Like a problem in a marriage, it took a while for it to build up into a full-scale row.'

Judy Huxtable says that Peter and Dudley were always independently asking her if she knew something about the other that they didn't. While the women were away, there was a good deal of competitive shagging. When Tuesday Weld joined them on tour, the atmosphere thickened. 'Peter and Dudley's obsession with each other increased,' she told Thompson. 'Whatever Dudley had for breakfast, Peter had to know. Whatever Peter was wearing, Dudley had to know.'

Behind The Fridge, which became *Good Evening* on Broadway, ran for four years, during which Peter married Judy on Valentine's Day 1974 in New York. Significantly, Dudley's place as best man was taken by Alexander Cohen. The tour ended with a six-week stint at the Schubert Theater, Century City, Los Angeles, from July to August 1975. Dudley and Tuesday had what they called 'a quiet wedding in Las Vegas' to which Peter was not invited, and then Dudley dropped his bombshell: he didn't want to work with Peter again. Peter knew that relations between them weren't what they had been, but he was still gutted at the split. From now on, Dudley would be a permanent resident of Los Angeles. he told Barbra Paskin that he spent most of the day at the piano, sometimes meeting producers, 'none of whom seemed to know quite what to do with this short, middle-aged man from Dagenham. "I suppose I was waiting for them to say, 'My God, you're the fellow we've been looking for!'" But of course it never happened.' Peter, meanwhile, was about to have what Judy described to Thompson as a nervous breakdown. 'For the best part of a year he couldn't eat or sleep. He just sat crying.'

On the album *Derek & Clive Come Again*, Cook found much of the emotion that is so strikingly missing from his screen performances, and if there is anger in his voice, it is not only anger at his volatile off-screen relationship with Judy Huxtable, but also at his extinct on-screen partnership with the man he affectionately called 'the little toad'. Take a sketch like 'I Saw This Bloke' from *…Come Again*. Cook is continually interrupting Dudley as he tries to start his sentence. Finally Cook says: 'You saw this bloke: any happier?' That, says the critic and biographer of Morecambe and Wise, Graham McCann, is a tiny moment of genius. 'Derek & Clive are underrated, but Cook's amazing rage at trivial things is extraordinary. He really means it.'

101

When, years later, Cook remodelled his Macmillan act to play a deranged prime minister called Sir Mortimer Chris in the film *Whoops Apocalypse* (released in March 1987) it was a fair effort, but his eyes seemed locked in a futile quest to elude the attentions of the camera. Behind shades, though, as he appears in the filmed version of *...Ad Nauseam* and *Derek & Clive Get The Horn*, Cook really lived those Derek & Clive moments, whereas Dudley acted himself out of the picture. Essentially, Peter Cook hogged the stage, or the microphone. The situation became so bad that when the pair were finally reunited, briefly and rather unsatisfactorily, in 1990, to introduce the surviving bits of *Not Only... But Also*, Cook ranted on at such a rate that he finally asked Dudley if he would like to get a word in. 'Yes', said Dudley. 'Very well', said Cook, 'What word would you like to get in?' 'Edgeways,' said Dudley, which was a perfectly valid point.

Dudley's clowning personality and his genuine desire to discover a character in somebody else's lines eventually made him, at forty-three, one of the most sought-after actors in Hollywood. In 1978, Dudley, acting alongside Goldie Hawn and Chevy Chase, portrayed a sex-mad musician called Stanley Tibbets in *Foul Play*. It is not a great film, but it was the springboard from which he went on to star in Blake Edwards' *10*.

Revisited in the Nineties, *10* is a forgettable late 1970s West Coast frolic, with too much pre-publicity centred on the cameo role performed by Bo Derek's breasts and some absurdly sentimental moral overtones. The whole tone of the plot, which revolves around ranking women from one to ten in search of the perfect specimen, is enough to provoke a thoroughly deserved rant from any self-respecting feminist, which should not be excused even in the different sexual climate of 1979. To quote *Time Out* film critic David Pirie, 'It's technically atrocious, trading on absurd coincidence, lame slapstick, and some peculiarly ugly photography.' And yet, as Pirie admits, it has its own weirdly seductive formula, helped by a delightful and unforgettable score from Henry Mancini.

Dudley's other great success, of course, was *Arthur*, which was released in 1981. Speaking purely personally, this writer thought it was unremittingly dire then, a view which the intervening years have done nothing to alter. *Arthur*, let us not forget, is the film which chose to have on the poster – *on the poster* – the line 'I race cars, I play tennis, I fondle women, but I have weekends off and I am my own boss,' which has long been my contender for the worst line ever spoken in a movie. The whole ethos of the film is staggeringly flawed: we are expected to feel sympathy for the dilemma of a poor little rich guy, a millionaire trustafarian who doesn't need to work, preferring to race toy trains in his bedroom.

He drinks champagne – brought to him by his butler, played with some semblance of dignity by John Gielgud – in the bath. A passing comment to a prostitute – 'Sometimes I just think funny things' – invites the obvious response from an audience of – 'Really? Why not tell us a few?' When *Time Out*'s Geoff Andrew described it as an 'overrated one-joke comedy' he was right on the money.

And there the matter would rest, were it not for the fact that, in both films, Dudley Moore comes across as sympathetic, romantic and – damn it – sensitive. Despite his duff lines – especially in *Arthur* – he proved with those performances that he could walk away from a mediocre movie having put in a star performance. Sadly for Dudley, he peaked with *Arthur*. True, he never quite scraped as low as *Wholly Moses*, which he made straight after *10*, but there was *Six Weeks* ('far-fetched... unconvincing' – *New York Times*), *Lovesick* (box office nose-dive), *Best Defence* (unremittingly awful), *Santa Claus – The Movie* (doomed) and *Blame It On The Bellboy* ('fairly bland' – Dudley Moore) – to say nothing of *Arthur 2*. Every time, though, there was no questioning the quality of the performance he turned in. Dudley knew exactly how to deliver a line. The fault was not his: the transition from sketch-performer to speaking other people's lines – that dream he had harboured for so long – made him reliant on script-writers, and he was badly served by them. He even boasted to friends that he never read his scripts until after he had signed the contract, which inflames some people's criticism of his agent Lou Pitt for not steering him away from unpromising parts, but Pitt insists that Dudley had no regrets about any of the flops. That's a shame for him, and for us.

Incidentally, Harry Thompson reports that when he was asked who inspired the role of *Arthur*, Dudley replied that he had based it in part on 'this man out there who's an alcoholic whom I know'. It can also not have helped Peter Cook that his own portrayal of a butler – in an American TV version of *Two's Company* called *The Two Of Us* made in 1981 and 1982 – won him considerably less popular acclaim than befell Gielgud, not least because his performance was so wooden. At least Dudley could speak other people's lines, no matter how bad they were. Cook simply couldn't. We can only conclude that Hollywood didn't take Peter Cook seriously as an actor because, unlike Dudley Moore, he couldn't take himself seriously as an actor. ■

chapter eIGHT
{celebrity, LA-*style* versus FAME, *nw 3*–STYLE }

> **Peter:** Of course, Buffy, one thing you
> will notice about Americans, God bless
> them, and that is, they are terribly naïve about
> sex… They just think of beautiful blondes with
> huge breasts and pink skins and blue eyes.
> **All:** Pathetic… yes, pathetic… very adolescent…
> absolutely pathetic.
> **Peter:** How do you think of sex?
> **Dudley:** I don't – at least, I try not to – otherwise I start thinking of
> beautiful blondes with huge breasts and pink skins…
> ('Home Thoughts From Abroad', *Beyond The Fringe*, 1962)

There are not, as we have observed, any entries from Dudley Moore in a standard twentieth-century dictionary of humorous quotations. Then again, the name of Peter Cook received scant coverage in *Hello!* magazine, which is a pity, as it would have been interesting to see what Cook made of *Hello!*'s 'English As A Foreign Language' interviewing style. Take the issue dated 25 January, 1992, just after Dudley Moore's separation from his third wife, Brogan Lane. The questions include: 'Dudley, you said your latest album, *Songs Without Words*, consisted of romantic and lyrical ballads. Is that how you were actually feeling at the time?' Or 'Would you say that you are a very sensitive person?' And (going for the

Peter and Eleanor Bron in Black Beauty, *1994*

jugular now) 'Would things have been different if you had been a little taller?' It almost makes one long for the delicate probing of a *News Of The World* doorstepper. Sadly, this is no time to debate *Hello!*'s contribution to international journalism, though it is worth noting that the cover stars of that issue, Elizabeth Taylor and Larry Fortensky ('Their love grows stronger every day') were acquaintances of Dudley's. In fact, the details of Dudley Moore's life have made the papers on both sides of the Atlantic, whereas Peter Cook eventually had to face the fact that he was a uniquely British cultural phenomenon. (The brilliantly perceptive obituary of Cook by John Lahr in the *New Yorker* doesn't count: editor Tina Brown was a Brit.)

This chapter is not only about the media's treatment of Pete and Dud at a time when they were inhabiting different worlds, but also about where they stood in the hierarchy of stardom. It is about the contrast between the 'fame' of Peter Cook, shuttling between Hampstead and Soho, and Dudley's West Coast 'celebrity'.

The last in the unholy trilogy of Derek & Clive albums, *. . . Ad Nauseam*, is one of the most unremittingly angry albums ever released. Although 'Horse Racing' and 'Sir' are sublime, most of it consists of Cook and Moore simply swearing their heads off at each other. As an example of the Primal Scream, it could have come straight from the sort of aggression therapy that Dudley was now increasingly drawn to in California. 'Never have two comedians slagged each other off so comprehensively,' was Cook's enthusiastic comment. Paul Donovan didn't count the number of times the word 'cunt' was used, and I don't propose to try, but it's a lot.

This partly stemmed from Cook's frustration at the knowledge that Dudley was walking out of his life to build a new one for himself in America. Cook hated not having Dudley around to bully, and the realisation that this really was the end ('Goodbye, sir, or is it *au revoir?'* 'No, Perkins,' from 'The Aftermyth of War', *Beyond The Fringe*) stung him. When, in *Derek & Clive Get The Horn*, Dudley dares to suggest that he is waiting for an 'edit point', Cook seizes on the filmic term to scream abuse at Dudley. 'Have you ever been in a movie then?' screams Peter at him, over and over, with Dudley forced to defend himself half-heartedly. The answer, of course, was that he hadn't been in any more films than Cook had, but he was about to appear in a lot more.

It is from this period that Cook started needling Dudley regularly about his exodus to California. ('It's the space, you see. He loves the space. Californians have a lot of space. Most of it's between their ears.') The trouble was, Dudley wasn't there. He was in California, as that *Beyond The Fringe* sketch had joshingly

Cook and Moore in 1973

predicted, having fun with 'blonde' (i.e. dumb, in Press-speak) women: Cook's jibes were falling on deaf ears.

In the late 1970s, Dudley was still trying to sort out his feelings about his damaged foot, and his stilted relations with his mother, and his extremely messy relationship with Tuesday Weld, by going in for some group therapy. It was during one such session, of course that he met Blake Edwards. Peter Cook was doing something similar at around the same time in Hampstead, by attending meetings of Alcoholics Anonymous at the behest of his wife Judy. He didn't get any work out of it, though Judy told Harry Thompson he did develop a rather funny impersonation of the man who ran the class, which at least made the other penitent drinkers laugh.

In 1977, when Dudley was commended to a young agent at ICM called Lou Pitt, he was just about to hit pay-dirt. Pitt says he sensed it: 'He was absolutely ready to explode,' he now claims. The two became friends, and Pitt became one of Dudley's most loyal lieutenants.

When he made *Foul Play* in November of that year, Dudley was paid $27,500 for three scenes. In November 1984, when shooting started on *Santa Claus – The Movie*, he was clocking up $4 million: that's a lot of reindeer. In fact, the best years of his career were over, but no one was to know that at the time, and the Press still delighted in pointing out that he was worth $16,000 per inch. In 1982, when

William Goldman was writing his classic primer *Adventures In The Screen Trade*, it would have been considered eccentric if he hadn't mentioned Dudley Moore. He quoted the Quigly list of the top ten stars of 1981. There was Dudley at number three, right behind Clint Eastwood and Burt Reynolds and nosing ahead of Dolly Parton, Jane Fonda and Harrison Ford.

Dudley bought an American house and he married an American woman. He was in love with America, and America loved him for it. At the end of 1978, the Hollywood Women's Press Club gave Dudley their coveted Golden Apple award for Male Discovery Of The Year. The runner-up was a certain Richard Gere, who has since gone on to scrape some sort of a career together. The best was just around the corner though. On the film set of *10*, Dudley endeared himself to cast and crew by playing the piano in between takes, as Cook had sought to entertain the cast of *The Wrong Box* all those years ago, albeit with considerably less success.

Almost immediately, the British Press started sniping at Dudley for selling out, going soft, or, to use a later phrase, dumbing down. Dudley had never denied that he preferred the American lifestyle. Besides, he wanted to pursue his acting career and his pregnant wife was American; it made sense for him to try life across the pond and he was not sad to say goodbye to England. 'Peter misses London,' he said while they were on tour in the States. 'Hampstead, the corner paper shop [sic], his mates. I don't. Not at all.' Dudley took to America, whereas Peter was always holding back. When Dudley had his Bentley imported to the States he had a personalised number-plate that read TENDRLY [sic]. There can be few more striking indications of the cultural chasm that yawned between the slightly soppy and sentimental Dudley and his astringent ex-partner. What number-plate would have done for Peter: CYNICLLY? When Hell froze over, perhaps.

{celebrity, LA-*style* versus FAME, *nw*3-sTYLE}

Almost every journalist on what used to be Fleet Street must have written an article at some time saying that Dudley Moore had 'gone soft'. He lived in a pink house down by the sea, and it didn't matter that it wasn't a very attractive beach or that blood from gang fights occasionally spattered the sidewalk, nor that sacrificed goat carcasses were sometimes found floating in the nearby canal. No, Los Angeles was home to a tribe of empty-headed sun-worshippers who spent all their free time with their analyst or giving barbecues on the beach. The famous, on-going 'nudie' party in *10* set the tone for how we imagined Los Angeles to be. Dudley had opted to join this community, indeed to be an enthusiastic proselytizer for it; therefore, it was assumed, he suffered from its worst excesses. Even Jonathan Miller indulged in one of his characteristic verbal lunges at LA: 'Los Angeles encourages people to indulge their wilder and more promiscuous forms of introspection,' the good doctor told Barbra Paskin, 'and then provides them with a terrible vocabulary with which to conduct their introspection. It's hard to distinguish Hollywood parties from group psychotherapy. It's the most stunningly vulgar town in the world. There's a free gas escape of nonsense that prevails, and people, if they go on breathing it, become brain damaged.' Despite that volley of abuse, Moore appeared in Miller's 1988 production of the *Mikado*, and both men got on very well with each other.

As for Peter Cook, who had knocked on Hollywood's door but had been refused entry, the headline writers were beginning to run away with the story. 'The star who was left behind when little Dud grew up into a giant,' mocked the *Express* in March 1982. 'For Pete's sake, come back Dud', the *Mail On Sunday* wrote in July 1984. There are few things the Press look forward to more eagerly than the sign of a successful man on the way down. And though the journalists couldn't help liking the man, if Peter Cook had got a tenner each time he was asked if he envied Dudley Moore, he would have ended up richer than his former partner. 'I do not envy Dudley his success going it alone in the States,' he kept repeating, until it began to sound as hollow as the Press no doubt intended it to.

In fact, Cook's friends thought him one of the least envious men alive, though he could not disguise his bewilderment at Dudley's new-found celebrity. To *Private Eye* colleagues like William Rushton, Cook could seem 'faintly furious' about Dudley's success. Richard Ingrams told Harry Thompson he sympathised with Cook's frustration at seeing Dudley celebrated for having skills which he felt he had in greater abundance. Dudley might never have been the wit that Cook was, but the world isn't always crying out for a mind as sharp as a blade, and for a while Dudley's softer, blander appeal was just what it wanted.

Before Dudley was swept up in the wave of publicity surrounding *10*, Peter had taken to phoning Suzy Kendall, and even Dudley's mother, to ask after his old friend. Peter also wrote Dudley this rather double-edged letter, reproduced in Paskin's biography, in which he ribbed him by accusing him of plagiarism. 'I had my hair permed before you did; I worry, you worry; I move to Hampstead, you move to Hampstead; I get divorced, you get divorced. Does this mean I'll be moving to the Marina?' The problem with the last line was that it was the wrong way round. Peter had not moved to the Marina to be followed by Dudley: Dudley had got there first. He had escaped: he was blazing his own trail now.

In February 1980, Peter flew to Hollywood, where he made no secret of the fact that he had come to look for work. Thompson tells the story – evidently true but so wounding that it should be apocryphal – that, as his taxi idled in heavy traffic on the way in from the airport, the driver got out to stretch his legs and walked past a few stationary vehicles, then turned and raced back to the car. 'Hey, you'll never guess who I just saw,' he shouted to Peter. 'It's Dudley Moore up there! *Dudley Moore!*' It was as if some mysterious force were striking Peter down for his hubris in daring to suppose he could ever equal his former partner's status.

Peter talked to some studio heads, but was sounding pretty defensive from the start. 'Yes I would like to be a sex symbol,' he said to journalists. 'Who wouldn't?' The trouble was, as Dudley said later, 'Peter was apologising all the time for being here and it showed in his work.' Peter did not have Venice Beach eyes, and he knew it.

At around the time Dudley was getting to know Hobson the butler (John Gielgud) in *Arthur*, Peter signed a deal committing himself to making *The Two Of Us* in the States. *Arthur* was an international hit, grossing over $100 million. After a promising start, CBS scrapped *The Two Of Us* in March 1982. And it was at just such a moment that the boys from the *Sun* chose to ask Peter if he regarded his career as a flop. 'My career is certainly not a flop,' he replied indignantly. We should not pause for too long to ask what character of person would ask such a question, nor what Cook had done to deserve having salt rubbed into his wounds like this.

In the coming months, he hit back by lashing out at Los Angeles' 'face-lifted androids' and he bemoaned its 'insufferable elitism and snobbery… People are only interested in what you are doing and they are always lying about what they are doing.' Dudley, by contrast, sounded bemused about why his old mate was still laying into him. Sometimes Cook snapped, as in this famous and quite sustained outburst, 'Perhaps if I had been born with a club foot and a height problem I might

Dudley with Nastassja Kinski in Unfaithfully Yours, *1983…*

have been as desperate as Dudley to become a star. That's all he ever wanted. I'm not trying to copy Dudley because I don't have the same need to prove myself.' The trouble with the campaign of attrition that newspapers conduct is that eventually, inevitably, you begin to sound as if you are protesting too much.

Dudley had his own battles to fight. As well as the constant search for spiritual peace, he was gripped by the usual actor's fear that he was only as good as his last review, or box office smash, and that he would never be able to top *Arthur*. Whereas Peter was always being asked if he would like to get back with Dudley (the answer to which was always, 'Yes, of course'), Dudley was always being asked where the next *Arthur* was (to which the answer was always a hopeful but unavailing 'In my next film'). He was also as committed a womaniser as ever, fulfilling the prophetic lines from *Beyond The Fringe* that opened this chapter.

Cook never lost his interest in the Press. Like many people in the public eye, he subscribed to a cuttings agency to keep a check on what had been written

... and with Daryl Hannah in Crazy People, *1990*

about himself , while Dudley once claimed he never read articles about himself 'unless the review is entirely in the nature of a genuflection', which was happening less and less.

Cook tried to quit London, but when he tried living in Exmoor with Judy in 1982 it lasted just two months. He missed London and his marriage to Judy was by now fatally flawed. Besides, if Devon was too far from Hampstead, what chance would he have stood in Los Angeles? Cook's notoriety was a London affair. He had his favourite restaurants like the Villa Bianca or La Sorpresa; his newsagent; the video shop. Cook famously claimed that 'My ambition was worn out by the time I was twenty-four.' He hadn't done all his best work by then, of course, as his partnership with Dudley was only just starting, but in his mind he was coasting from then on. Something similar happened to Dudley twenty years later. After the double hit of *10* and *Arthur*, Dudley too was coasting: a minor hit here, a good-ish concert there, but effectively his best work was done in a feverish three-year patch. Dudley fought it, and like the one-legged man in

'One Leg Too Few' refused to believe the worst. Peter, on the other hand, seemed to revel in the laurels he had earned, and was sitting on. Once a star, though, always a star, even if you're a fallen star. When Dudley came to London for Peter's memorial service in 1995, he was the man the Press went after. It is always better to be a visiting celebrity than a resident celebrity: like the Pope, the less Dudley came to Britain, the more keenly his brief appearances were anticipated.

Cook continued to alternate between lashing out at Dudley and sounding happy for him, which left Dudley bemused. 'I never wanted to be a "star",' said Dudley. Jonathan Miller agrees. According to Miller, it was Peter not Dudley who craved stardom. 'Peter always longed for that type of showbusiness success. He wanted to be a movie star and envied Dudley that particular success.' By 1980, Cook was pouring cold water on his old hankerings. 'At one time I had the idea of doing romantic leads. But I looked such a berk I couldn't carry on,' he told the *Mirror*, defensively.

For most of the 1980s, Dudley Moore was living the sort of life in Hollywood that people read about in magazines while they're having their hair done. Barbra Paskin records that his friends included Glenn and Cynthia Ford, Peter Bogdanovich, John Huston, Jane Fonda and David Hockney. He and Brogan went for dinner at Tina Sinatra's, or Liza Minnelli's. Jackie Collins would ask them over for dinner, and they once went out for a meal with Bob Dylan at the chic restaurant Chasen's. There were parties for Blake Edwards and dinners with Joan Rivers in Bel Air. In another spasm of life imitating art, he rented the former home of Greta Garbo, whom he and Cook had metamorphosed into Emma Bargo back in 1970. It was as if Dudley was living out the fantasy life that he and Pete used to snigger about from behind their fists. Take one of Peter's lines from *Derek & Clive (Live)*: 'But I'll tell you one thing Tony Newley said to me: "Who are you?" Just like that. And I thought that made Tony Newley a wonderful human being.' Ho ho, very cutting. A few years later, Dudley and Newley would be sitting side by side on a chat show.

Cook had his showbiz mates, too. He played golf with Bruce Forsyth, Jimmy Tarbuck, Michael Parkinson and Kenny Lynch, as well as many golfing professionals. Then there was Frankie Vaughan, Terry Wogan, Bobby Charlton, Michael Winner… It was a different league from the guests who used to come to dinner with Peter and Wendy in the swinging Sixties: Lennon and McCartney, Charlotte Rampling, Peter Sellers, Peter Ustinov, Michael Foot, Cat Stevens. Whereas Peter and Judy had been quite self-contained, big names still came for dinner with Peter and Lin, though it was less a 'scene' thing.

unveiled in the Hollywood Walk Of Fame, next to that of Louis Armstrong. Dudley had proved he was still one of America's most successful immigrants. Cook, meanwhile, had his own routine. To an interviewer as mediocre as Hunter Davies, whose most probing question was to ask Peter to list his top ten hobbies, he insisted that 'he was perfectly content. He had no ambitions. None at all.'

Both men spent much of the 1980s in a sort of goldfish bowl. Peter retreated to his Queen Anne house in Hampstead and dedicated himself to daytime TV and developing an astonishing expertise in the most esoteric programmes. In a way, he was turning into a British Andy Warhol: a one-time dandy with a taste for populist gestures who reinvented himself as a lover of all things trashy, a man who could not be shocked, a man with his finger on an off-beat cultural pulse, who gloried in the very things he derided and was fêted by succeeding generations, many of whom only had a vague notion of what he had done in the first place.

Dudley, meanwhile, proved convincingly that celebrity had not made him any happier. He ricocheted between various women, from the kind and well-meaning Susan Anton to the generous, home-making Brogan, but his terror of commitment prohibited him from enjoying the fruits of his labours and his neurotic philandering sabotaged one decent relationship after another. Professionally, he knew it was over. A few years later, in October 1995, he told Douglas Kennedy of the *Mail On Sunday*: 'Look at the careers of most actors. If they're lucky, they're top banana for five years, no more. I was tops for around two years. And then, one morning, you wake up and find you've been shifted onto another list. You're no longer an A-list actor. You're now on the B-list… and falling.' Nor did it end there. ∎

Peter and Dudley again in 1989

chapter nINE
{drink *versus* drugs }

Pete: Mr Woolley was a very nice family man with a lovely wife and two beautiful children… One evening, he came home and looked around and said, 'Nice though this be I seek yet further kicks.' After that… his cravings got worse and worse. He got more and more drugs down his face, and eventually he became so irresponsible, he left his lovely wife and kids and home behind and went to Hollywood and lay on a beach all day with a lovely busty starlet with blonde hair what came down to her knees.

Dud: That doesn't sound too bad, Pete.

Pete: No, I don't think that's a very good example of the perils, actually.

(From the 'Beeside' of 'The L.S. Bumblebee', 1967)

There used to be an ancient society at Cambridge called the True Blue Dining Club. It was closed down some years ago in mysterious circumstances – probably due to the loud and boorish behaviour of its well-born, high-spirited members – but the Minutes books provide a snapshot of several centuries of extremely drunk undergraduate activity. The main event of each evening's bacchanal was, of course, a drinking contest. Each member in turn would be given a decent bottle of claret, and a silver bucket was placed reverently between his – never her, of course

Dudley and third wife Brogan Lane at the Oscars, 1988

– feet. The member would haul himself upright, down the bottle in one go, and then, with the secretary's eye on his stop-watch, the seconds would be called out until the inevitable happened and he threw up into the silver bucket, whereupon, amid great whoops of delight, the interval between consumption and evacuation was carefully noted and the member collapsed in a heap on the floor. In about 1961, a distinguished former member was welcomed back for one of the society's feasts. If memory serves, the note went something like this: 'Mr Peter Cook delighted us with his presence, and showed us that he had lost none of his natural wit.' A note was scratched in the margin against his name: 'nine seconds'.

Although towards the end of his life there were long periods when he didn't touch a drop, and he steadfastly attended a health farm twice a year, by the 1980s, anyone who read a newspaper – and Peter Cook read them all – knew that the Press had made up its mind about Cook. Newspapers are wary of complexity: just like the writers of *The Wrong Box* and *Monte Carlo Or Bust*, they preferred to work from a few basic assumptions and, in the case of Peter Cook, it came down to: (1) Best work behind him (2) Misses Dudley (3) Drinks.

Admittedly, Peter Cook was making it easy for them. When *Private Eye* nearly folded in May 1989 over the threatened libel award of £600,000 in favour of Sonia Sutcliffe, the girls and boys from the Press knew they only had to walk Peter round the corner to the pub, sit him down and order the drinks, and pretty soon they'd have a story. Then, of course, they'd be off back to their offices to write it up in an affectedly sanctimonious style, leaving Cook where he preferred to be, which was in the pub.

Peter Cook had at times been no stranger to 'uppers and downers' when depression overwhelmed him, according to his second wife Judy Huxtable, but his alcoholic past is even better documented. Dudley always says it started at the beginning of the *Behind The Fridge* tour in Australia in 1971, when Peter – crazed to hear from Wendy that his second daughter Daisy had had an asthma attack in London – keeled over from drink and fell, fully clothed, into a hotel swimming pool. Then there was the first night of *Behind The Fridge* in London in 1972 when the curtain couldn't go up for about an hour because he was so drunk. And there were the times during that tour when Dudley tried to talk to Peter but found his partner sobbing silently, creased up with drink. No wonder Dudley didn't turn into an alcoholic: Peter's behaviour was enough to put him off drink for life.

Heavy drinking puts friends in an invidious position. Some, like Richard Ingrams, were reformed drinkers themselves who regretted that Peter 'wasn't quite sharp'. It was all very well for friends like Barry Humphries to say 'If Peter had managed to stop drinking he would have been a thousand times funnier', but – unlike Humphries – Peter had patently not managed it. His friends must have felt like Charles Ryder in *Brideshead Revisited*, watching the beautiful Sebastian Flyte subsiding into alcoholism. Ultimately, what could you do with someone who was that determined to drink, except pour their drinks and think 'poor Peter'? Cook almost never became a nuisance, though former *Private Eye* man Martin Tompkinson recalls one alcohol-fuelled fight with him in his early days on the magazine. Ian Hislop, who took over as editor after Ingrams retired in March 1986, admitted to Harry Thompson that, 'To be honest, if Cookie was pissed it was a complete waste of time.' Other insiders like Barry Fantoni, Dave Cash and the late John Wells insisted that, even when he was very, very drunk, Cook was still gallant, and very funny.

Dudley's career was in crisis throughout much of the 1980s, though so much of his energy went into his sexual appetites that brewer's droop was the last thing he could afford – ironic, considering his success as the permanently sloshed Arthur. After *Arthur* he made eleven films in that decade, but his constant search for the right part was perpetually frustrated. His search for the right partner should perhaps have ended with Brogan Lane, to whom he was married from 1988 to 1992. She did all she could to care for him, but in the end his kicking out against the love of a good woman sent yet another marriage crashing.

Peter had more luck with his third wife. He married Chinese-born Lin Chong on 18 November 1989, and got from her the comfort and support he needed. He was still trying to come to terms with the separation from Judy, the woman he had referred to as the love of his life. Lin was a different person, someone who had missed all the craziness of the 1960s, who had no association with that period or those people. She preferred the gentle meanderings of EL Wisty to Derek and Clive's catarrhal expletives, and after his death she became a zealous keeper of the flame, often to the annoyance of the rest of Cook's family, but while she may have tried to draw a veil over some aspects of his private life, there is no denying that Lin became the love of Peter's later life. She, more than anyone, tried to act as a go-between with him and Dudley, apologising to Dudley on Peter's behalf for those caustic remarks that she was sure were never intended as harmful. After her intervention they talked on the phone a lot more and left each other answerphone messages. Peter would have jumped at the chance to work with him again, of course, and he asked him several times, but the harder Dudley found it to get the right part in Hollywood, the more he was convinced that if he teamed up with his old partner again it would seem like stepping backwards, which was not a sensible signal to send out to any casting director.

The only times they teamed up together now were for one-off shows or interviews. Whenever they did, Dudley would be dressed in a modest suit with hair carefully brushed, as if he were on his way to a board meeting, while Cook, in an ill-fitting jacket and T-shirt, looked as if he had just been thrown out of a pub. It was as if Dudley was actively indicating that this was just one of several things he had to do in a busy day, while Peter seemed happy to admit that he had nothing much else planned for the rest of the week.

William Donaldson, who brought *Beyond The Fringe* to London in 1961, has revised his opinion of the Peter Cook who enchanted 1960s Britain. 'He had one character with a silly voice, and he had *Private Eye* which was anti-intellectual and xenophobic, and that's all. He wasn't the most talented member of *Beyond The Fringe*: Jonathan Miller was. But everyone just bowed down in front of him.' He adds that, during Cook's latter years, any project with his name on it was dead in the water owing to his reputation for drinking. Back in the early 1990s, though, the mercurial Donaldson and Cook staved off the unendurable ennui by taking

Cook the tennis player

Ecstasy, which Peter swore would make Donaldson fond of Richard Ingrams. (It didn't work.) Donaldson also says that Cook took a lot of cocaine, but he adds that 'I think the fact that he was an alcoholic saved him from being into much harder drugs,' just as the fact that Dudley was a sexaholic saved him from becoming an alcoholic. Each to his own.

While Dudley Moore was doing a well-paid advertising campaign for Tesco, Cook had an account with his local off licence and packed away a lot of champagne, wine and vodka. Dudley built up an impressive collection of upmarket wine. In Paris, he and Brogan sniffed and sipped an 1899 Lafite, which Dudley was amazed but not embarrassed to hear cost $1,000. Refined eating and dining had become second nature to Dudley, while Peter rarely ventured beyond La Sorpresa or the Villa Bianca – no slur on those fine restaurants intended – at the end of his street.

The author of this book remembers seeing him stride into the Coffee Cup – another favourite Hampstead haunt – late one evening in about 1983, eyes gleaming, face perspiring, clearly not just back from a jog on the Heath. He sank his teeth into a cheese toastie, destroying it in about fifteen seconds, and then swept out again, leaving the other coffee drinkers whispering 'Wasn't that Peter Cook?' in hushed tones.

The one time we spoke, I sat with him in his front room, waiting for him to extemporise a review of a new Spike Milligan biography. He seemed quite calm, and only occasionally sipped from a can of lager, while almost ignoring the cigarette that smouldered between his fingers. He was friendly and encouraging, but he said he could only review the book if someone was there to take notes while he flicked through the pages looking for something to fire his imagination. The year was 1988, and he seemed utterly exhausted, like a man who had heard every joke ever made. When I got home, I was disappointed at how little material he had actually produced, and how I had proved to be no substitute for Dudley Moore.

Whenever Dudley talked about home, or Peter Cook, it was as if he needed to be reminded about the world he had left behind. For Cook, though, there was no shortage of reminders, an endless line of journalists eager to quiz him on Dudley's latest movie, or girlfriend. And the most frequent question was: when was he going to get back together with Dudley? If only he had replied as Dudley had done in the 'War Correspondent' sketch from *Goodbye Again* (1968), when Peter, as the correspondent, asked Dudley, as the Sergeant, a typically inane journalist's question. 'Completely off the record and in total confidence, of course,' said

Dudley in a harsh Scottish accent, 'my considered response to your interesting question is "Shut your face or I'll stuff your teeth down your windpipe."'

The media behaved towards Cook as they did towards all icons – like a child playing with a fragile toy. They toss it up into the air to see if it smashes, and when it doesn't they toss it up again. They keep on doing so until eventually, of course, it smashes, whereupon they howl because their toy is broken. For Cook, the master of improvisation, it must have been paralysing to have nothing more recent than 'One Leg Too Few' (aka 'One Sketch Too Many') to perform whenever he was reunited with Dudley, or to have to dig up Sir Arthur again. And yet when he was creatively blocked he fell back on his bankers, like said 'One Leg Too Few'. It suited the media that they could refer to Cook as 'the former satirist' or 'ex-partner of Dudley Moore': they didn't want anyone to rock the boat by straying from the script. Media reputations are usually built on whatever the last journalist found in the cuttings file, thus endorsing what has already been said.

Of course, pretending that Cook just liked the occasional 'half' is fatuous. Richard Ingrams sensed a 'muddiness' in Cook's later years that he said stemmed from drink. In fact, both Cook and Moore were increasingly powerless to prevent a creeping dissatisfaction stealing over them, which left them listless and overcome by depression, but which they coped with in different ways: Cook with booze when the going got rough, Dudley with a combination of sex and some drugs. Cook was probably an undiagnosed manic depressive. Dudley was unable to enjoy the fruits of his success while the going was good, and tortured himself with anxiety when the good times had gone. 'Dudley always had angst,' his first wife Suzy Kendall told Barbra Paskin. 'He couldn't exist without it.' At least Dudley had twenty-four hour TV with which to console himself. In the days before television spread to occupy every available hour, Peter Cook viewed the empty stretches as anxiously as if it were an empty glass. It was intolerable, being thrown back onto himself for so long. At least Dudley could talk to his therapist or play some music. Peter was left concentrating solely on himself.

In 1987, Cook played a cameo role in *Mr Jolly Lives Next Door*, directed by Stephen Frears. It starred Adrian Edmondson and Rik Mayall, with Cook in a slashing role as the psychotic neighbour. It isn't a great film, but it marked the beginning of Peter's rehabilitation, thanks to the rise of a generation of comics suckled on the sour milk of Derek & Clive. Now that they were fast becoming the new comedy establishment, they gladly acknowledged Cook as their hero, and cast him accordingly. Dudley, meanwhile, worked with comedians like

A very unusual Fringeship

Eddie Murphy, Robin Williams or Chevy Chase (who wisely observed to Barbra Paskin that 'Comedy is about making people laugh'), many of whom knew entire Pete and Dud or Derek & Clive routines by heart. Peter Cook appeared on topical programmes like *Have I Got News For You* where he could indulge his passion for the latest ephemera. But the sober intervals between binges were slowly being imbibed away. Would the real Peter Cook stand up? Often he couldn't.

A decade earlier, he had agreed to Judy's request that he attend Alcoholics Anonymous meetings. Alan Bennett, quoted by Harry Thompson, suspected Cook wouldn't be able to keep it up, 'simply because his sense of the ridiculous is so strong that he won't be able to get through the meetings'. Bennett had been proved right. Interviews referred repeatedly to him 'lounging' or 'dishevelled', 'sprawled', or 'slouching'. As the 1990s dawned, Cook went on swinging wildly between alcohol and abstinence. At one stage his weight ballooned to 16½ stone, his hair was grey and unkempt, his face looked flabby and his voice sounded raspy. One of the terribly sad things about being a chronic alcoholic is the lengths to which heavy drinkers sometimes go to pull themselves back from the brink. Peter had always been an enthusiastic golfer, though Michael Parkinson recalls seeing the contents of Peter's golf bag: it was filled with cans of Bacardi and Coke. 'After about four holes he was pissed. I think we made it round to the tenth, by which time he didn't know where he was,' he told Harry Thompson. He had always been a keen tennis player, but, as Alan Bennett almost said, there was always a little bottle of vodka in the corner of his life. That, and a cigarette burning. It wasn't that his friends and admirers disapproved, or felt he should 'sort himself out'. They were just scared he was going to kill himself.

Friends wondered fearfully what was going to get him first: cirrhosis of the liver or cancer of the lung. It would have been a strange ending for the man who had so biliously raged against the dying of the light. Without Paul Donovan's help we can only guess at how many times the word 'cancer' was repeated on the Derek & Clive albums, but it was a high enough number. The song 'My Old Man's Got Cancer', to the tune of 'My Old Man's a Dustman', was a taboo-shattering tour de force, because it dared to confront a subject that many people were still profoundly uncomfortable discussing. In the post-Aids era, the power of cancer to scare has decreased considerably, but the subject was just not discussed openly in those days, and Cook and Moore's persistent references to it went a long way toward desensitising us to it, just as, in the previous decade, Cook's Macmillan impersonation shattered the myth of prime ministerial infallibility.

We didn't realise it then, but Cook was also touching on a private taboo, since Dudley's father had died of colonic cancer in 1971. Harry Thompson says Peter knew that perfectly well, of course, and that it had been 'the single most devastating event of Dudley's life to date.' Barbra Paskin quotes Dudley's sister Barbara as saying, rather mutedly, 'Dudley felt a lot of regrets when my father died… He was very saddened,' which just proves that you can't measure out grief in easily grasped units.

The years 1993 and 1994 were surprisingly busy for Peter Cook. His marriage to Lin gave him a solid domestic base for the first time in many years. There was a very successful launch party for the *Derek & Clive Get The Horn* video in September 1993, which proved that getting lots of big names together works spectacularly better for parties than in films. The guests included some Rolling Stones, a few Pythons, Alan Bates, Ian Dury, Dave Stewart, David Gower and many others. 'It was probably the happiest I ever saw Peter,' Rainbow George Weiss later told Andy Beckett in the *Independent On Sunday*. 'He'd have been quite happy to die that evening.' Cook also recorded a *Clive Anderson Talks Back* 1993 Christmas special in which he turned in one of his best performances ever, playing four versatile and well-observed characters and proving that he had finally learned to be reasonably comfortable in his own body on camera.

In November 1990, Peter had teamed up with the multi-talented John Lloyd and Peter Fincham to make a programme for TalkBack, the company started up by Mel Smith and Griff Rhys Jones on the back of their inferior Derek & Clive 'Head to Head' pastiches, and which has gone on to make some of the best comedy programmes on TV or radio. Cook, as Sir Arthur Streeb-Greebling, was interviewed on camera by Ludovic Kennedy about the twelve days of Christmas, under the title 'A Life In Pieces.' It was a somewhat guarded performance by the two grand old men, but Cook as Sir Arthur was put through his paces by an altogether more coltish newcomer, Chris Morris, on a version of 'Why Bother?' recorded for BBC Radio 3 in 1994. Morris's lack of awe towards Cook's Streeb-Greebling is monumental, and Cook is audibly pushing himself to maintain Morris's relentless pace. At one stage Sir Arthur asks if he can tell a story about bees. 'It's quite an interesting anecdote, actually,' says Cook. 'It sounds dull to me,' sniffs Morris. Cook, startled at this insolence, lurches on. 'I had some bees in my youth and put them to work making honey,' he says flatly. 'Mmm,' says Morris and moves on. This, surely was Morris's 'Herr Nurrr' moment: at a stroke, he swept away the very basis on which Cook first made his name, of improvising endless apian monologues to giggling admirers. Listening to it, one felt the same shock that a loyal Macmillan acolyte would have experienced having accidentally strayed into the Fortune Theatre in 1960.

Peter's well-being closely mirrored that of his adored mother, and although he had seemed fitter than he had been for years in December 1993, when she died on 6 June 1994 Peter went to pieces again. Knowing his limits, he had checked himself into hospital several times over the years to give his liver a rest, but he could not save himself. He died on Monday 9 January 1995.

Dudley was interviewed several times over that period. He was clearly flattened, wiped out by the news, and his gift for analysing comedy – never one of his strong suits – was obviously at full stretch. Struggling to order his thoughts, he stammered his way through one interview after another: 'He just created an extraordinary sense of fun... There was something extraordinary about his ability to pooh-pooh any altar... He did what he wanted and to hell with anybody else. He used to appear on Hampstead High Street in his slippers: he didn't mind how he was interpreted...' At first sight, there was something admirable about the way he didn't succumb to waves of sentiment and pronounce Cook the kindest man he had ever known, or was there? Dudley's mind was darting in strange directions, and the TV news presenters struggled to keep him on track. Was his refusal to be nostalgic a sign of shock, or was it memory loss?

Dudley's contribution to Lin Cook's festschrift, *Something Like Fire*, was conducted by interview with the combative journalist Christopher Hitchens. Dudley admitted to Hitchens that his memory was 'poor and incomplete', and when asked to reminisce about their film appearances Hitchens drew another blank. 'A favourite anecdote? No. A particular memory? No. An act of kindness or generosity? No.' He admitted to journalists feeling 'puzzled and rather hollow' about Cook's death but added, 'It wasn't unexpected, let's face it.' When Harry Thompson interviewed him for his biography of Cook, he found 'a terribly nice chap but I had far more idea of what he was doing than he had. He thought *Not Only... But Also* was in 1974 and Derek & Clive was in the 1960s.' Thompson didn't say what had caused Dudley to become, in Richard Ingrams' words, 'muddy', but it was evident that the reason was not just to do with the blanket of grief that had settled around Dudley's shoulders after Peter's death.

During the late 1980s, Dudley had experimented occasionally with 'disco biscuits', more commonly known as Ecstasy (as he told Barbra Paskin). They performed the useful function of taking Dudley Moore's mind off Dudley Moore. He also tried amphetamines. Recreational drugs are traditionally the province of pop bands and others with a preternatural capacity for getting up late the next day, so it wasn't a great idea for Dudley to discover them at some time in his fifties, but Ecstasy was a promiscuous party guest in the late 1980s before some of its side-effects (like death) were known.

Dudley Moore had enjoyed a brief affair with a seventeen-year-old girl called Nicole Rothschild in the mid-1980s. After Brogan moved out of his Marina house in 1989, Nicole became a regular visitor and eventually they became lovers. Apart from a year or so when Dudley was seeing Quincy Jones's daughter Jolie in 1992, Nicole was the woman in his life. He adored her, at least as far as he was able to. 'Unfortunately I don't know what the word love means but I *think* I love Nicole,' he told one journalist. To another he said, 'Nicole is great for me and at last I've met someone who is terrific.'

In March 1994 Nicole and Dudley had a fight. Each of them phoned the police, and eventually Dudley was led off in hand-cuffs. He was released a few hours later on $50,000 bail for what the LAPD called 'cohabitational abuse' or 'spousal battery'. The two made up the next day, however, and Nicole was showing off the marks on her neck, amid intense press debate about what had caused them. It certainly beat Cook's worst run-in with the police, when he had drunkenly wrapped his car round a lamp-post. The pair, now labelled by the media as 'Hollywood's most dangerous couple', got married three weeks later, though they retained separate houses. Five months later, Nicole's former husband Charles Cleveland moved into Nicole's house, he claimed, to act as a paid nanny to his own children. Dudley did not need to star in a sitcom about a man who is in a bizarre relationship with some ex-spouses. He was in one anyway. (Interesting headline-related footnote. *Daily Mirror*, July 9, 1994: Dudley on 'Why I can't live with the woman I love.' *Daily Mail*, November 12, 1994: Peter Cook on 'Why my wife won't live with me.')

Nicole wanted a baby but she and Dudley weren't having sex, so they opted for artificial insemination, and it worked. Meanwhile, Dudley paid for all Charles' medical bills. Then Dudley left the Marina house he had lived in for twenty years and moved one hour south of Los Angeles to join Charles, Nicole and the extended family in Corona Del Mar. After a tiff in August 1995, Nicole rang the London papers – whose fading interest in Dudley was now mainly prurient – to tell them she and Dudley had separated. The following day they were back together. The pattern repeated itself in October. In November 1995, after only one day on the set of Barbra Streisand's new film *The Mirror Has Two Faces* – the film which Dudley half-hoped would mark his return to acting – he was sacked for repeatedly getting his lines wrong.

Cook and Lin in Covent Garden, circa 1988

Newspapers on both side of the Atlantic continued to print unsubstantiated stories concerning Dudley and Nicole, detailing rows, slanging matches, and screaming fights conducted between street and balcony. In public, however, Dudley continued to be positive about his relationship with Nicole. 'All is domestic bliss and tranquility,' he said in October 1995. 'The sun is shining, my marriage is fine.'

When allegations were made about the domestic life of Nicole and Dudley, they made puzzling reading. What on earth were newspaper readers to make of the claim that Dudley had given Nicole the dollar equivalent of £1,200 a month for one of her five sisters to water his plants? Was it all a vicious slur on the photo-synthesising capabilities of their bougainvillea? Peter Cook himself could not have invented a more surreal tale.

In fact, Dudley's old partner occupied less and less of Dudley's waking thoughts. 'At some point, I'll forget that I ever worked with Peter Cook, I suppose,' he said to a journalist in 1995. He was also developing a worrying tendency to remember banal aphorisms and repeat them to visiting reporters – 'Sometimes I think music is the one thing which makes me happiest,' was one. 'I don't know what happiness is…maybe it's nothing more than a by-product of a moment in time', was another.

In the third week of December 1998, Dudley flew back to to Los Angeles. He had been absent since September 1997, when he had undergone open-heart surgery. Now he wanted to see his house, which he missed. He also saw Nicole. After Christmas the friends he was staying with were going to England. Dudley joined them for the flight, which was when the photographs appeared of him walking with a crutch, a nasty gash disfiguring his face. The picture even appeared in *Hello!*, the magazine which had previously alleged nothing more damaging than the suggestion that his album *Songs Without Words* consisted of romantic and lyrical ballads. Newspaper articles then started to appear with headlines such as 'Downfall of Dudley Moore'. It all sounded like a chapter from Kenneth Anger's *Hollywood Babylon*, or some apocryphal Derek & Clive track. People were comparing Peter's last days with what were assumed to be Dudley's (wrongly, as it turned out). Peter drank himself to death, it was observed, but at least he knew he was loved by Lin. To the media, it all seemed to suggest that chronic alcoholism was less dangerous for one's health than Dudley's relentless pursuit of Hollywood stardom and starlets.

There was a sketch on the 1968 show *Goodbye Again* in which Dud had his palm (or his left foot) read by Mrs Woolley. He told Peter, with some alarm, that 'she said I was not long for this world'. Pete reassured him by explaining that she had meant that he was 'on the short side'. The explanation seemed to satisfy Dud. Now, though, thirty years later, were Mrs Woolley's words about to be proved right at last?

As I flicked guiltily through the latest tittle-tattle in the nation's downmarket press one morning, I got a phone call from a publisher. Would I be interested in writing a book about Pete and Dud – the double act? 'Give me a second to think about this… yes,' I replied. Had I met Cook?' Once or twice, very briefly.' And Moore? 'Well, it depends on what you mean by "met".' 'You know,' the publisher continued, 'Have you been to his house?' It was a straight choice: Dagenham or Los Angeles. I rang Trailfinders.

chapter tEN
{dud's coNclusion }

Topped and tailed by mountains, Los Angeles is where the desert meets the ocean. The traffic sweeps smoothly along the freeways, the sun feels closer, and the women…
Driving in from the airport along Sepulveda Boulevard, the air smells sweet like bubble gum – though it could be smog. I wanted to explore that seductive paradox, that dangerous double act, for myself. It was the last piece of the jigsaw, the topping out of the Cook/Moore double act. I had heard enough about collagen implants to swell my expectations. I wanted to see for myself the place that Dudley Moore had chosen for his home. Of course, if he wanted to sound off for several hours about life, love and Peter Cook, I'd be happy to listen, but somehow I didn't think I was going to get that chance. In short, if Dudley Moore's life had become the stuff of journalists' clichés, I was tired of reading them: I wanted to write a few myself.

Los Angeles is famous for living on the edge, of which the most graphic example is the San Andreas Fault. Dudley had had his house reinforced against the constant threat of an earthquake, but that was a trifling risk compared to the upheavals that rocked the foundations of his private life. When Peter Cook died, there was much debate about what contradictory messages he had sent out in the last years of his life. Sure, he had drunk colossal amounts to numb the pain of divorces, artistic failures and disappointments. But his last few months had been

Dudley the film star, 1988

relatively vigorous. He had been together with his daughters Lucy and Daisy at Daisy's wedding in September 1994, which was a very happy, simple occasion and he had even talked contentedly to Wendy for the first time in twenty-five years. It was true that Lin's relations with the rest of Cook's family were far from warm, and went rapidly downhill after his death, but at least she had always been there for him, which is surely the best anaesthetic you could want when facing eternity or nothingness. Compare that with Dudley's condition: Unwell, face marked with a nasty gash, walking with a stick, isolated and withdrawn from his old circle of friends. Was this all the result not just of his terminal promiscuity and an overdose of marital spats but also of his low self-esteem and an occasional but persistent need to cut himself off and keep the shutters drawn?

Dudley's divorce from Nicole Rothschild was finalised in November 1998. There seemed to be an awful historical inevitability behind it. And now, only a few months later, Dudley was lying low somewhere, physically frail, hiding from his ex-wife, his friends, and the world. And, of course, the world's press. Was this to be the sad closing scene to a glory-strewn life, or was I being sucked into the media myth surrounding Dudley's life, just as an uncomfortable part of me felt I had ben drawn down the tabloids' glamorously sleazy and factually selective version of Peter Cook's death?

It was in Los Angeles that the dream that was Pete and Dud finally ended. When the curtain came down on the last night of *Good Evening* at LA's Schubert Theater in 1975, Dudley told Peter that this time it really was over, and this time he meant it. They stuttered and stammered every once in a while after that, and they came together for brief stints to make their famous smutty triptych, but effectively the partnership was dead. Dudley left Peter in Los Angeles in 1975, and he was still there, where the party had ended, almost twenty-five years later.

It took many years for him to say so, but Peter eventually admitted that the split had left him 'bereft... It produced a gap in my life which is probably still there today. When people asked "What are you going to do now?" I really didn't know.' The schism with Peter was painful for Dudley, too, but it was positive pain, as Dudley was making his first moves in the movie world, and had just married for the second time. By the time his fourth marriage came crashing down around him, Dudley was in perhaps more pain than ever before. Peter used to joke that Dudley spent years trying to find himself. In the end, though, had Dudley finally lost himself? As I arrived in Los Angeles, I was fearful of what I might find.

Francis Megahy was lunching in one of his favourite cafés, the Coffee Bean And Tea Leaf on Sunset Boulevard. A live wire who looked years younger than a sixtysomething, it was clear from the innocently animated way he was chatting to the blonde woman on his left that here was a soulmate of Dudley Moore. I sat down opposite him and switched on my tape recorder. This was base camp, LA.

Megahy had been at St Paul's School with Jonathan Miller, but he had got to know Dudley in 1958 or 1959 while he was making films and living in the West End and Dudley was playing jazz. He saw *Beyond The Fringe* many times, met Bing Crosby in the dressing room one night, and sat one seat along from Jack Lemmon at the opening night of the Establishment. Peter Cook's question and answer sessions as Harold Macmillan at the Establishment were a *tour de force*. Could he remember any of it? 'Not a word, I'm afraid, but *TW3* was totally bland by contrast.' What were Cook and Moore like in private? 'Peter was harder to get to know than Dudley. I was meant to be having dinner with Wendy once but she couldn't make it so I dined alone with Peter,' he said. 'Very tricky: not an easy man to be on your own with.'

How about Dudley? 'Just delightful. Really funny, spontaneous, charming, a brilliant musician and wicked with the ladies.' And with Peter? 'Together they were brilliant. They'd do a fifteen-minute warm-up for *Not Only… But Also* that was just… brilliant.' Could he…? 'Not a word, but it was brilliant.' Has he seen Dudley recently? He paused. 'Not for a long time. A year, maybe more. I'm worried about him. If you see him, send him my love.'

Dick Clement, who produced the second series of *Not Only… But Also*, is looking fit and healthy, having moved to LA with his writing partner Ian La Frenais and their wives. He sits at a pink-clothed table in the breakfast room of the Beverly Hills Hotel and picks at a bowl of Granola. 'It was about the most creative three-month period of my life. They'd work out their Pete and Dud dialogues, and I'd just give it an incredibly light touch on the tiller and that was it. Those studio tickets were the hottest tickets in town. It was like a party: everyone wanted to be there. Peter was so brilliant, but he would probe until he'd found your weak spot. On his own he was slightly cold. He needed Dudley's warmth. We used to go off and film on the Monday and we didn't even have a finished script. They'd just improvise, and it was brilliant, brilliant.' Had he seen Dudley recently? 'Not for, well, a couple of years. It's very sad. The downside of being swept up by fame so quickly is that when the tide goes out it's doubly cruel. But what a lovely guy. I can still hear his laugh in my mind's ear.'

I had an enjoyable drink in the same place with their old friend and fellow Brit Peter Bellwood. He writes and teaches film, wears a narrow leather tie, and ducked outside occasionally for a crafty smoke. He hadn't seen or heard from

In an ideal world. . . Dudley with girls unlimited in 30 Is A Dangerous Age, Cynthia *(1968)*

Dudley for a while either. I also met the remarkable Ms Paskin, wearing golden slippers in her book-lined apartment with line drawings of her by David Hemmings on the wall. We drank Moroccan sunflower tea while the very cockatiel which had once picked at the threads of Dudley Moore's shirt did the same to me. I made several calls to Dudley – numbers that other people had given me – but was told in a variety of polite American accents that I was barking up the wrong tree. I had a great, garrulous hour or two with British-born writer, producer and, latterly, humorist Martin Lewis, who talked a lot about the later projects he had overseen such as the Amnesty International shows and Cook's brief stage reunion with Dudley. He also maintained that the duo's 'Psychedelic Baby' ditty on the 1966 *Private Eye* Christmas flexidisc was the world's first song to refer openly in its lyrics to the emerging psychedelic craze. Then it was time for some Americans. I went to see Lou Pitt, Dudley's long-time agent and now manager.

Lou Pitt is also one of Dudley's longest-standing friends. His job is to defend Dudley Moore and he adores him with the same childlike enthusiasm that he had when he first met him. 'He was just this incredibly bright, soulful, funny, irreverent person. Women adored him because he was so outrageous and so silly. He'd walk into a room and it would just light up.' Is it still there, I asked. Long pause. 'It's not where it was.' Could he get it back? An interminable pause. 'I don't think you ever get anything back if you lose it, or if it changes, which is a roundabout way of saying that nobody ever is what they were; it becomes different.'

Lou thinks Dudley was a clown, but in a positive way. He thinks Dudley trusted the Press too much at times, sure, but reckons 'he talked about what he felt he needed to talk about.' And yes, some films didn't work, but 'no one person makes a movie, it's a real collaborative process.' This was going really well.

How about his womanising? Was that a good thing? 'I never judged him, it was none of my business.' But did he ever have any regrets? 'None that I knew of; at least he never voiced any. He accepted responsibility; he did what he wanted to do and chose to live his life and his career the way he wanted to.' Great. Is he happy? 'Oh yeah, absolutely, I think he feels lucky and fortunate and I think he feels that he accomplished an incredible amount and was very well rewarded, emotionally and otherwise.'

Dudley really liked Lou. In 1981, after the success of *Arthur*, he took an entire one-page advertisement in *Variety* to thank Lou for looking after him, a gesture which I didn't feel like copying at the end of our interview. And, yes, of course he was in touch with Dudley, but he wasn't saying where he was. I got back in the car and drove up into the Hollywood Hills where, just round the corner from Kevin Costner's place, Dudley's third wife Brogan Lane now lives.

She's still beautiful, and funny, and she's lost none of her height. She's an interior designer, starting with her exquisite house, which she's completely refurbished – a bit like what she tried to do with Dudley but with more pewter basins pillaged from defunct churches. She clearly loves Dudley very much, and when I suggested that she was still angry at him, she hotly denied it. She last saw him about eighteen months ago, when fears of a brain tumour proved to be wide of the mark. How was he? 'He couldn't really have a conversation. He falls down, talks about things out of context, slurs. It's almost…' She remembers Dudley's self-pitying poem I had shown her. 'It's almost as if now he really is a fly without wings and legs. So I said to him: "You are now at a time in your life where you really, really have to look at yourself and the world in a very different way, because there are a lot of things you can't do."

'He used to have a recurring dream of burglars coming into his house and stealing everything in it and just smiling while they're taking everything out, like furniture removal men. And he would be, like, "What are you doing?" And then, like, "Oh, don't mind." He was always the victim.'

So what was it like being married to Dudley Moore? 'Whenever we flew somewhere we had the limo picking us up; we had guys with walkie-talkies saying, "They're coming in." They would take us from the car, literally walk us to the gate, handle everything… I'm telling you, after eight years of that I truly was frightened of going to an airport, parking my car and catching my own plane.'

Brogan had tried to get him to be more physical 'and not just stay mental the whole time.' She took him skiing, where he had to expose his foot so that it could be waxed. 'That took a lot, that was gutsy,' she says. On the other hand, she rented a villa on an island so that they could run around bare-legged and Dudley wouldn't have to worry about other people seeing his deformity. ('Your right leg I like. I have nothing against your right leg. The trouble is….')

Brogan says: 'Dudley was never easy to be with, there's no doubt about that.' And why did he get involved with Nicole? In Brogan's opinion, it was 'Because she was probably the first person who never really gave a shit. And you know what happens with that: you try harder to get them to love you.'

Brogan maintains that Dudley was never actually unfaithful from the time of their marriage to their eventual separation. She is still scathing about the illicit relationship she suspects he had with one of his female therapists, though she balks at naming her. And is she still cross that Dudley seemed unable not to give his number to pretty girls? 'No, but I used to say, "Do you know how many men would like to know what I am about? And do you know how often I could give my number out?" But he never got it.'

She didn't get to know Peter Cook well. By the time she was on the scene, Peter and Dudley's conversations were 'guarded, and seemed all surface talk.' Eventually she 'caught' part of Dudley's depression, simply because she was exposed to him so much. 'I was always trying to fix him; he was my project,' she says. 'He was high maintenance, that son of a gun – and he thought *I* was high maintenance!' I thanked Brogan and said goodbye. It was time to go to the beach.

Dudley's restaurant at 72 Market St. is a sleek, airy brasserie in glass, steel, slate, concrete and oxidised metal, with art decorating its creamy walls. The maître d' said Dudley was in there every day of the week before Christmas. Was he playing the piano? 'No,' he said defensively, 'but he seemed OK.' Since the New Year, though, they hadn't heard a word from him. I bought the Market St. book, with its seventy-two recipes (banana squash ravioli looks good, as does roasted squab with candied garlic and green lentil ragout), and drove the mile or so to the Marina.

As if the melancholy that was already sweeping over me needed further elaboration, it was raining when I got there. Dudley's house, which he bought in 1977 and was formerly owned by the comic actor Rudy Vallee, is modest by West Coast standards. It is perched on the edge of an unassuming strip of sand, shoulder to shoulder with its neighbours but for a narrow stretch of path on one side. Directly behind it was that rather grimy stretch of beach across which Dudley had raced Nicole – watched with some bemusement by her two kids from her marriage to Charles Cleveland – on the day of their wedding in 1994. The Press always claimed it knew they'd had an argument when Nicole came out and stood on the balcony, while Dudley's piano music could be heard wafting from inside as he tried to woo her back, or console himself. These days the house is still pale pink, the same colour as the table-cloths of the Beverly Hills Hotel, the colour that made the British Press think Dudley had 'gone soft'. It doesn't shout 'movie star'. The cameras over the doors are pretty standard for the better-heeled parts of LA. The front door is of rounded wooden beams, and the first of the house's three floors is covered with a blue moon-shaped awning. With the sun shining on it, it might look like pretty, but on a soaking day in mid-winter and a stiff wind playing havoc with the volleyball nets a few hundred yards away, it looked as miserable as an abandoned wedding cake.

A young man appeared at the gate next door. Did he live here? Yes. He knew who his famous neighbour was, right? 'Well,' said the man, 'they say it's

Dudley Moore but I haven't seen him for at least eighteen months, maybe longer.' But he used to see him? 'Well he used to drive his car up and down the street, but now...' Did any Press ever come over to see the house, take a look, take photographs? The man bit his lip and shook his head. Not any more. It was very quiet; indeed, he thought the house was totally uninhabited. ('She's so uninhibited!' 'She's so unin*hab*ited,' as Peter and Dudley once warbled in happier days.) He asked me what I was doing. I told him I was writing a book about Peter Cook and Dudley Moore. he stared back at me blankly. 'Peter who?' he asked. 'Dudley's partner,' I said. 'His former partner.' 'Right,' said the man, uncertainly. 'Was he British?'

I had a final look at the forlorn pizza delivery flyer hooked over the door handle, and the traditional 'Armed Response' placard, and, pausing only to curse whichever traffic cop had penalised me for parking on Pacific Avenue before 12pm on a Tuesday, drove the five hundred yards to the house on Hurricane Street that Dudley had bought for Nicole.

It was a similar colour, though on a smaller scale, and outwardly more messy. A date palm and a picket fence in the front garden, and a load of junk left out in which pools of water had collected. There was a bird cage, an old barbecue ('Hamburger stands but no fucking hamburgers' – from *Derek & Clive Come Again*) a doll's house and a plastic kiddies' hut. There are few more distressing sights than children's possessions left out in the rain. The windows were shuttered, and – I'm projecting here, obviously, but – a sort of spiritual stasis, even paralysis, seemed to radiate from behind those windows, as impenetrable as George Spiggott's shades in *Bedazzled*, as if a light had been flicked off and the darkness allowed to flood in.

The back of the house was even more nondescript than the front, save for the abandoned paddling pool that lay in two kinked halves by the garage. I strained my ears to hear the vestiges of the blood-curdling rows that used to electrify the air, but caught nothing.

Adopting for a moment the old journalistic stand-by known as 'pressing the doorbell', I did so, and was surprised to find a male voice answered. Obviously it wasn't Dudley, but at least someone was in. I explained who I was, half-expecting an Armed Response crack squad to come screeching round the corner. To my surprise, I was admitted to the downstairs room by a man in his early twenties (Dudley's son Patrick was 23 this year), who said in a laid-back voice that he was 'a friend of Nicole's', and allowed me a few minutes to snoop. It barely made any difference, because the house was an empty shell. The shutters were down and the light was soupy, even in mid-afternoon. My host said Nicole was away and then turned his attention back to a small TV set, where some cartoon characters were blasting each other's heads off. He was sleeping in a sleeping bag. There was a packet of biscuits on the floor, an alarm clock – presumably to remind him when it was time to go to bed – and that was it.

There was a tasty-looking French-style armchair, a neat little Swiss-style wooden chandelier over the dining room table, a slatted wooden staircase at one end, and a step down to a well-equipped kitchen at the far end of the house that looked as if it hadn't ever really been put through its paces. I tried to imagine the moments of tenderness there had been round that table, rather than the screaming rows. It was a bit like one of those studio tours that all the major film companies offered, except that nothing was in production. Once again, Stanley

A dapper, greyer Cook

Moon's words to George Spiggott in *Bedazzled* came back to haunt me, with Nicole standing in for Peter Cook. 'I like you, but you keep on doing these terrible things…'

I asked him his name. 'Patrick,' he replied. Patrick? Was he Dudley's son? 'No,' he said, 'I'm just a friend of Nicole. You're not going to take any pictures are you?' Oh well, it was worth a try.

I left, and drove ruminatively around a marina that was glinting with sails before rejoining the San Diego freeway. I only had one day left in Los Angeles, and it didn't look as if I was going to get my three-hour intimate chat with Dudley – not that I had seriously expected I would. I thought back to Lou Pitt's blandly reassuring words and mentally tossed them out of the window. If Dudley was satisfied with his life, my name was Stanley Moon.

My mind ran through the closing track of ... *Come Again*, a free-form sketch which began as a distinctly off-colour conversation between a Streeb-Greebling type and a husky-voiced troglodyte, cottaging in a gents' toilet. After the initial filth and squalor have died down ('I am a private club: I can only admit one member a day,' says Peter), Dudley decides he's having a heart attack, whereupon the conversation goes off at the most bleakly apocalyptic tangent.

> **Peter:** What's it like to die?
> **Dudley:** Well hold on a moment. It's not as bad as you might think... but not as good either. I'll tell you what I'm afraid of.
> **Peter:** What's that?
> **Dudley:** Absolutely everything.
> **Peter:** Good night, darling.
> **Dudley:** Good night, my darling.

I should come clean here: I had always been a 'Cook man' in the past. With his apparently effortless mastery of language and timing, Cook's name was the one most people pulled out when the word 'genius' was bandied around, and I – like the rest of the *Beyond The Fringe* cast – had tended to under-value Dudley's creative input. But during my short stay in Los Angeles, and despite not getting anywhere near him, Dudley's life had made much more sense to me. He didn't just play the satyr to Cook's sometime satirist, and he was much more than Peter Cook's straight man. He was the lightning rod that earthed Cook's unpredictable bolts, but he had his own brilliance too. Not only that: he had uprooted himself to come and live here, had embedded himself in the affections of the most inward-looking but entertainment-crazy country on Earth, and his on-screen warmth had provided the most distinguished moments in some otherwise undistinguished films. No doubt about it: Dudley Moore was here. He had left his mark on the desk. Unfortunately, somebody had left their mark on his cheek too.

The trouble with being one half of Derek & Clive was that, having enfranchised proletarian culture as they did, they seemed so accessible. You felt you could just march up to Dudley, quote the words of Peter Cook from ... *Come Again* ('I said, "Come on, Norm, drink up, don't be a cunt..."') and the two of you would amble off to the nearest pub and everything would be alright. But given the epic, gothic calamity of Dudley's downfall, magnified and broadcast by the media – at times with the collusion of the protagonists – it is impossible not to feel profoundly moved by Dudley's tragic fall from grace. I was lucky with this book. Often, when you meet someone who is writing about some famous figure, you ask what they were like and the writer responds, through gritted teeth, 'Arrogant, pompous, vain conceited, by all accounts impossible to work with: a total bastard.' The two men I was writing about were total opposites, but they were both immensely popular. Everybody, even (most of) their ex-wives, loved them. The trouble was, it wasn't until Peter Cook died that his real popularity could be gauged. Was that going to have to happen to Dudley too?

Their work is their memorial, from Dudley's choking hysteria in the art gallery or the zoo ('During the winter months his RRRs blew off') to the immortal Bargo parody. They delighted in smut while also revelling in the innocent pleasure of songs like 'Isn't She a Sweetie?', 'Alan A'Dale' or 'Goodbyeee'. They left us some intriguing films, and some great television programmes (sadly, only a fraction of their overall output remains, as the BBC wiped most of the series). The absurdism of this marriage of opposites created the foreground for *Monty Python's Flying Circus* in the Sixties, and their taboo-shattering, scarcely-concealed vehemence anticipated – and largely paved the way for – what became known as alternative comedy in the 1970s, years before Alexei Sayle put on his first pork-pie hat. For years, Pete and Dud were a private joke that the whole nation was in on. So what if, as people said, in the end they had under-fulfilled their potential. Hadn't both of them vastly over-fulfilled it in the beginning?

At the beginning of this book I quoted Peter Cook's description of his relationship with Dudley Moore as a marriage. A surfeit of marriages eventually proved to be Dudley's undoing, and yet without that initial engagement to Peter Cook, he might well have been just another family entertainer. I thought back to the first reference in BBC history to Dudley Moore. It was from Joanna , then the BBC's Head of Television Programme Planning, and it was sent to Donald Baverstock, Assistant Head of Light Entertainment (TV) on 18 September 1959. It read as follows:

> 'Please may I commend to you Dudley Moore (publicity piece attached) whom I saw perform at this year's Edinburgh Festival. His line is topical songs at the piano, and he struck me as most talented. I am finding out where he can be reached, and will send the address on as soon as I have it.'

{Pete & Dud}

Dudley Moore's whereabouts were no mystery in those early days, especially to a young woman. By contrast, I only found out where Dudley was lying low in America when I was safely back in London. How times had changed.

The ability to be funny, or to create humour, derives from viewing the world with a squint. Great double acts possess a rare chemistry, in which their contrasts create something that the audience can agree on, namely laughter. Peter Cook and Dudley Moore were a study in opposites, even down to their final days, but during their years together they created a timeless, rich and varied body of work. Peter Cook's tragedy was that he died relatively young; perhaps Dudley Moore's tragedy was that he didn't. But my final wish is that he will enjoy a riper, more contented retirement, and that it will still be a while yet before he is reunited with his old sparring partner to continue exploring their unique incongruity. ■

1966, on the set of Not Only... But Also

BIBLIOGRAPHY

Dudley Moore is, at the last count, the subject of four biographies. The first, by Jeff Lenburg, is no longer available over here but caught the initial tone of Dudley's rise to stardom after *10* and *Arthur*. The second, by Paul Donovan (*Dudley*, W.H. Allen, 1988) plods over the same ground reasonably diligently. *Dudley Moore* by Douglas Thompson (Little, Brown, 1996) has little new to add. The 'official' biography by Barbra Paskin (Sidgwick & Jackson, 1997) eclipses the others through its detail and for the frankness with which Dudley spoke to the author. It is at times over-reverent, and better at analysing the marriages than the shows, but there is no escaping the poignancy of its final chapters.

Peter Cook has only received the biographical treatment once, but Harry Thompson's magisterial book (Hodder & Stoughton, 1997) is unlikely to be surpassed for some time. Thompson turned up a vast amount of material which threw new light on Cook, his work, his wives and his relationship with Dudley and, apart from the odd historical quibble, it's a gripping read. Other books that cover the same period include Lin Cook's collection of tributes to Peter Cook in *Something Like Fire* (Methuen, 1996) now renamed *Peter Cook Remembered* (Penguin), John Hind's *The Comic Inquisition* (Virgin, 1991), a fascinating series of interviews with great comedians including Peter Cook, Ronald Bergan's *Beyond The Fringe... And Beyond* (W.H. Allen 1989), a diverting and perceptive look at the four members of *Beyond The Fringe*, and Roger Wilmut's seminal *From Fringe To Flying Circus* (Methuen 1980). There is also, of course, *The Complete Beyond The Fringe* (Methuen), *The Dagenham Dialogues* (Methuen). And so on.

DISCOGRAPHY

NOT ONLY PETER COOK... BUT ALSO DUDLEY MOORE
(Decca LK4703) 1965
The Ravens. Superstitions. Tramponuns. Art Gallery. Initials. Religions.

ONCE MORE WITH COOK
(Decca LK4785) 1966
Dud And Pete On Sex. Father and Son. The Frog And Peach. Six Of The Best.
The Music Teacher. A Bit Of A Chat. Dud And Pete At The Zoo. The Psychiatrist.

BEDAZZLED
Music from the film soundtrack.
(Decca LK4923) 1968
Main Title. Moon Time. Strip Club. Italy. The Leaping Nuns' Chorus. G.P.O
Tower. Love Me*. Bedazzled*. The Millionaire. Sweet Mouth. Cornfield.
Goodbye George. Lillian Lust.
(Selections Composed by Dudley Moore, *Cook/Moore.)

GOODBYE AGAIN
(Decca LK4981) 1968
The Trial. Long Distance. Mrs Woolley's Curse. Aversion Therapy. Workout.
War Correspondent*. (*with Rodney Bewes)

NOT ONLY BUT ALSO
(Decca LK5080) 1970
Dud Dreams. In The Club. Lengths. This Is Ludwig Van Beethoven.
The Making of a Movie. 0-0 Dud.

BEHIND THE FRIDGE
(Atlantic K40503) 1973
Hello. On Location. Mini-Drama. The Gospel Truth. Tea For Two. (Recorded
at the Cambridge Theatre, London, 1973. Directed by Joe McGrath.)

GOOD EVENING
US only release. (Island 9298) 1975
Hello. One Leg Too Few. Madrigal. Mini-Drama. Six Of The Best.

{Pete & Dud}

The Frog And Peach. Die Flabbergast. Gospel Truth. (Record at Plymouth
Theatre, New York, 14.11.73. Directed by Jerry Adler.)

ALL THE ABOVE TITLES WERE DELETED AT THE TIME OF WRITING (JUNE 1999)

THE BEST OF PRIVATE EYE: GOLDEN SATIRICALS PRESENTS VOLUME ONE – THE FAMOUS FLEXIES
(MCI GAGDMC085)1998
Double-tape release collecting *Private Eye* magazine's give-away flexidiscs from
1964 to 1980. Prominent appearance by Peter Cook alongside John Wells,
Willie Rushton, Barry Fantoni, Barry Humphries et al. Dudley performs on the
mid-60Is discs, most notably as Spiggy Topes of the Turds Pop group, being
interviewed by Peter (As Eamonn Andrews) and singing 'I'm a Red Hot
Swinging Perve'.

THE COMPLETE BEYOND THE FRINGE, WITH ALAN BENNETT, PETER COOK, JONATHAN MILLER, DUDLEY MOORE (AND PAXTON WHITHEAD)
(EMI 7243 8 54045 2 8) 1996
Written by the cast. A 3-CD compilation of the complete London Show, 1961,
directed by Eleanor Fazan, with music by Dudley Moore, recorded 16 & 17
May 1961, plus selections from the Broadway production, recorded January 27
1964, with Paxton Whitehead as Jonathan Miller.

PETER COOK AND DUDLEY MOORE PRESENT DEREK AND CLIVE (LIVE)
Island ILPS 9434) 1976. Currently available on CD (IMCD7)
The Worst Job I Ever Had. This Bloke Came Up To Me. The Worst Job He
Ever Had. Squatter and the Ant. In The Lav. Little Flo*. Just One Of the Songs*.
Winky Wanky Woo. Bo Dudley*. Blind*. Top Rank*. Cancer*. Jump*.
Taped at Electric Lady Studios, New York,1973. (*Taped at The Bottom Line,
New York, 1973.)

DEREK AND CLIVE COME AGAIN
(Virgin V2094) 1977. Currently available on CD (CD0VD110).
Coughing Contest. Cancer. Non Stop Dancer/My Mum Song. Joan Crawford.
Norman The Carpet. How's Your Mother? Back Of The Cab. Alfie Noakes.
Nurse. In The Cubicles. Ross McPharter. Hello Colin. Having A Wank. I Saw
This Bloke. Parking Offence. Members Only.

The CD version has the additional tracks: You Stupid Cunt. Valerie's Hymen*. Mother*. Films. Young Dudley Moore performs 'Jump'*.
(*Taped at ...*Come Again* album sessions.)

SINGLES BY PETER COOK & DUDLEY MOORE
(Decca F12158) 1965
Goodbyeee/ Not Only But Also (Instrumental by The Dudley Moore Trio)

THE BALLAD OF SPOTTY MULDOON/ LOVELY LADY OF THE ROSES
(Decca F12182) 1965
Technically a Peter Cook 'solo' single, but both tunes credit Cook and Moore as composers and The Dudley Moore Trio provide the backing

BY APPOINTMENT E.P.
(Decca DFE8644)1965 45 rpm

ISN'T SHE A SWEETIE?/BO DUDLEY
(Decca F12380) 1966 45 rpm

THE L.S. BUMBLEBEE/ THE BEESIDE
(Decca F12551)1967 45 rpm

BEDAZZLED/LOVE ME
(Decca F12710) 1967 45 rpm

VIDEOGRAPHY

THE BEST OF... WHAT'S LEFT OF... ONLY... BUT ALSO...
(BBC V4430) 1990
Ninety-minute compilation preceded by a special 'emotional reunion' of Pete
And Dud. Contents: Nowhere Edgways (1990). Birmingham To Mandalay Bike
Race (1970). A Spot Of The Usual Trouble (1965). Bo Dudley (1966). The
Making Of A Movie (1970). A Bit Of A Chat (1966). Primitive Painting (1966).
At the Zoo (1966). Super Thunderstingcar (1966). The Tale Of Alan A'Dale
(1965). The Glidd Of Glood** (1970). Bargo (1970). Tower Bridge (1970).
Tramponuns (1965). French Guide To The North Circular*** (1965). Ludvig
Van Beethoven (1970). Art Gallery (1965). Goodbyeee (1966). Material
written by Cook and Moore except *Bob Sale,** Cook, *** Robert Fuest & Joe
McGrath.

THE SECRET POLICEMAN'S BIGGEST BALL
(Columbia TriStar Home Video) 1993
Film of Amnesty International gala at Cambridge Theatre, London, August 30 -
2 September 1989. Includes Cook & Moore's last stage appearances together,
performing 'One Leg Too Few' and 'The Frog And Peach' for the last time.

DEREK AND CLIVE GET THE HORN
(PolygramGram 0864663) 1993
One and a half hours of footage shot during the ...Ad Nauseum album sessions at
town House Studios, 1978. Material includes: Mother. The Horn. Sir. Records.
Hamster Reincarnation. Horse Racing. Marriage. Endangered Species. Jump.
Drug Bust. I Wish I Could Boogie Like Uncle Tom. Soul Time. Dancing in the
Park. Labels (alternative Take). Stripper.

FILMOGRAPHY

PETER & DUDLEY AS ACTORS ONLY, UNLESS OTHERWISE STATED:

THE WRONG BOX
(1966) Produced and directed by Bryan Forbes. Screenplay by Larry Gelbart.
Cast includes: Ralph Richardson, John Mills, Michael Caine, Nanette Newman,
Peter Sellers, Tony Hancock, Wilfred Lawson, Cicely Courtnedge, Irene
Handl, Gerald Sim, John Le Mesurier.

BEDAZZLED
(1967) Based on an original idea by Peter Cook and Dudley Moore. Screenplay
by Peter Cook, music and songs by Dudley Moore. Cast includes: Eleanor
Bron, Barry Humphries, Raquel Welch, Michael Bates, Alba.

THE BEDSITTING ROOM
(1969) Produced and directed by Richard Lester. Screenplay by John Antrobus
and Charles Wood, based on the play by Spike Milligan and John Antrobus.
Cast includes: Rita Tushingham, Dandy Nichols, Spike Milligan, Michael
Hordern, Roy Kinnear, Arthur Lowe, Frank Thornton, Ronald Fraser, Harry
Secombe, Ron Moody, Jimmy Edwards, Marty Feldman.

MONTE CARLO OR BUST
(1969) Produced and directed by Ken Annakin. Screenplay by Jack Davies,
Ken Annakin. Cast includes: Tony Curtis, Susan Hampshire, Terry-Thomas,
Eric Sykes, Jack Hawkins, Hattie Jacques, William Rushton, Gert Frobe.

THE HOUND OF THE BASKERVILLES
(1977) Produced by John Goldstone, directed by Paul Morrissey. Screenplay
by Peter Cook, Dudley Moore, Paul Morrissey. Music by Dudley Moore. Cast
includes: Irene Handl, Denholm Elliott, Joan Greenwood, Terry Thomas, Max
Wall, Kenneth Williams, Dana Gillespie, Roy Kinnear, Prunella Scales,
Penelope Keith, Spike Milligan, Jesse Matthews.

PETER COOK'S SOLO FILM PROJECTS

ALICE IN WONDERLAND (1966)
FIND THE LADY (1976)
THE SECRET POLICEMAN'S OTHER BALL (1982)
YELLOWBEARD (1983)
THE SECRET POLICEMAN'S PRIVATE PARTS (1984)
SUPERGIRL (1984)
WHOOPS APOCALYPSE! (1986)
MR JOLLY LIVES NEXT DOOR (1987)
WITHOUT A CLUE (1988)
GREAT BALLS OF FIRE (1989)
GETTING IT RIGHT (1989)

DUDLEY MOORE'S SOLO FILM PROJECTS

30 IS A DANGEROUS AGE, CYNTHIA (1968)
ALICE'S ADVENTURES IN WONDERLAND (1972)
FOUL PLAY (1978)
10 (1979)
WHOLLY MOSES (1980)
ARTHUR (1981)
SIX WEEKS (1982)
ROMANTIC COMEDY (1983)
LOVESICK (1983)
MICKI & MAUDE (1984)
BEST DEFENSE (1984)
UNFAITHFULLY YOURS (1984)
SANTA CLAUS THE MOVIE (1985)
LIKE FATHER, LIKE SON (1987)
ARTHUR 2: ON THE ROCKS (1988)
THE ADVENTURES OF MILO AND OTIS (1989)
CRAZY PEOPLE (1990)
BLAME IT ON THE BELLBOY (1991)
PARALLEL LIVES (1994)
THE DISAPPEARANCE OF KEVIN JOHNSON (1995)
A WEEKEND IN THE COUNTRY (1995)

Holmes (Cook) and Watson (Moore) sitting on a pile of trouble in The Hound of The Baskervilles, 1977.

CHRONOLOGY

1935 Dudley Moore born, Charing Cross Hospital, London 19 April.

1937 Peter Cook born, Torquay 17 November.

1946-54 Dudley to Dagenham County High School.

1951-56 Peter educated at Radley.

1954-58 Dudley to Magdalen College, Oxford.

1957-60 Peter to Pembroke College, Cambridge.

1960 *Beyond The Fringe*, The Lyceum, Edinburgh.

1961-62 *Beyond The Fringe*, Fortune Theatre, London.

1961 The Establishment Club admits members for the first time, 5 October.

1962-64 *Beyond The Fringe*, Golden Theatre, Broadway.

1962 Peter becomes joint proprietor of satirical magazine *Private Eye*.

1963 The UK Establishment Club is hosted at the Strollers Theatre Club in New York for the first time, January.

1963 The Establishment Club closes its doors for the last time 23 September.

1963 Peter marries Wendy Snowden, 28 October.

1964 Lucy Cook born to Peter and Wendy, 4 May.

1965 *Not Only... But Also.*
Seven 45-minute shows broadcast fortnightly from 9 January to 3 April.
Directed by Joe McGrath. Four shows still exist.

1965 The US Establishment Club closes for good.

1965 Daisy Cook born to Peter and Wendy, 10 September.

1966 *Not Only ... But Also*
Seven 30-minute shows broadcast weekly from 15 January to 26 February.
Directed by Dick Clement. Two shows still exist. (A Christmas Special directed by John Street and transmitted on BBC2 on Boxing Day 1966 also still exists.)

1967 Peter appears in *Alice in Wonderland* (BBC). Producer: Jonathan Miller.

1968 Dudley marries Suzy Kendall, 15 June.

Four one-hour specials for ATV broadcast 18 August, 24 August and 14 September (directed by Shaun O'Riordan) and one in 1969 (produced by Garry Smith and Dwight Hemion). All shows reported to be in existence.

1970 *Not Only... But Also*
Seven 45-minute shows broadcast fortnightly from 18 February to 13 May on BBC2, Cook and Moore's first series in colour. Directed by Jimmy Gilbert. All material filmed in the studio has been destroyed. All that survive are specially filmed sequences such as 'Bargo' and 'The Glidd of Glood'.

1970 Dudley and Suzy separate.

1970 Peter and Wendy formally separated, May.

1970 Dudley stars in *Play It Again, Sam*, Globe Theatre, London.

1971 *Behind the Fridge*, Australia.

1971 *Peter Cook and Dudley Moore In Australia*
Two 30 minute shows made for Australian station ABC broadcast 12 and 19 February. Both shows exist.

1971 Peter hosts *Where Do I Sit?* (BBC2), Feb-March.

1972 *Behind The Fridge*, Cambridge Theatre, London.

1972 Dudley and Suzy Kendall divorced.

1974 Excerpts from *Behind The Fridge*
Abysmally edited 45-minute version of their stage show, filmed at the Cambridge Theatre, 1973. Shown on BBC2 on 7 March.

1973-75 *Behind The Fridge* is retitled *Good Evening*, previews in Boston, then at the Plymouth Theatre and tours the USA.

1974 Peter marries Judy Huxtable, 14 February.

1975 Dudley marries Tuesday Weld, 20 September.

1976 Patrick born to Dudley and Tuesday Weld, January.

1976 *Saturday Night Live* US TV, transmitted 24 January. Peter and Dudley are special guests and perform 'One Leg Too Few,' 'The Frog And Peach' and 'Gospel Truth' as well as appearing with regular SNL crew.

1978 Peter hosts *Revolver* for ATV, July–September.

1981 Dudley and Tuesday Weld divorce.

1986 Peter appears on *Can We Talk?* with Joan Rivers.

1988 Dudley marries Brogan Lane, 20 February.

1988 Peter and Judy Huxtable divorced.

1988 Dudley in Jonathan Miller1s Los Angeles production of *The Mikado*.

1989 Peter marries Lin Chong, 18 November.

1990 Dudley stars in *Orchestra* (Channel 4) with Sir Georg Solti. Producer: Jonathan Hewes.

1990 Peter records *A Life In Pieces* with Ludovic Kennedy.

1990 *The Best Of...What's Left Of...Not Only...But Also*
Six 30-minute shows compiled form surviving footage of 1965, 1966 and 1970 series, screened by BBC2 November-December.

1992 Peter stars in *Gone To Seed* (ITV).

1992 Dudley and Brogan Lane divorced, September.

The Post Office stamp celebrating Peter Cook's contribution to Britain's comedic heritage

1993 Dudley makes *Concerto* (Channel 4) with Michael Tilson Thomas. Producer: Jonathan Hewes.

1993 Peter appears on *Clive Anderson Talks Back Christmas Special*.

1994 Dudley marries Nicole Rothschild, 16 April.

1994 Peter records 'Why Bother?' with Chris Morris.

1995 Peter Cook dies, 9 January.

1995 Nicholas Anthony born to Dudley and Nicole Rothschild, 28 June.

1998 The Post Office issues a series of stamps bearing caricatures of the nation's favourite comedians drawn by Gerald Scarfe. Peter Cook's likeness adorns the most expensive (at 63 pence) 23 April.

1998 Dudley and Nicole Rothschild divorced, November.

The full range of Post Office stamp celebrating Britain's comedic heritage

PICTURE CREDITS